WORK-LIFE BA

CU00456691

Based on a thorough review of the research on work-life balance, Sirgy and Lee identify a set of personal interventions that selected employees commonly use to increase their work-life balance and life satisfaction. Personal interventions of work-life balance involve five behavior-based strategies and four cognition-based strategies. The behavior-based strategies are engaging in multiple roles and domains, increasing role enrichment, engaging in behavior-based compensation, managing role conflict, and creating role balance. The cognition-based strategies are segmenting roles and domains, integrating roles and domains, engaging in value-based compensation, and applying whole-life perspective in decision-making. This volume provides HR managers and HR consultants with pedagogical material designed to help them develop in-house workshops, seminars, and curricula for their employees to improve their work-life balance by using the personal interventions described in the book.

M. JOSEPH (JOE) SIRGY is a management psychologist. He received his Ph.D. from the University of Massachusetts (1979). He has published extensively in the area of business administration, business ethics, and quality of life, and he has received many awards over the years for his research, teaching, and service to the management discipline. He has co-founded the International Society for Quality-of-Life Studies, the Macromarketing Society, and the Community Indicators Consortium. He served as editor in chief for *Applied Research in Quality of Life* and the *Journal of Macromarketing*. He also served as co-editor of several book series related to quality of life and human wellbeing and published numerous books on quality of life and human wellbeing.

DONG-JIN LEE is a professor at the School of Business, Yonsei University, Seoul Korea. He received his Ph.D. from Virginia Tech (1996) and has published extensively in the area of quality of life studies. Before joining Yonsei University, he was on the faculty of the University of Western Australia (1996–1999) and the State University of New York at Binghamtom (2000–2002). He served as Vice President for Academic Affairs, Vice President for Publication, and Program Area Chair for the International Society for Quality of Life Studies (ISQOLS) in 1997–1999, 2007–2009, and 1997–1998 respectively; he was Section Editor of *Applied Research in Quality of Life* (ARQOL) from 2009 to 2011; and he was Dean of Sangnam Management Institute at Yonsei University from 2017 to 2018. He won the best paper award from ARQOL in 2021.

WORK-LIFE BALANCE

HR Training for Employee Personal Interventions

M. JOSEPH SIRGY

Virginia Tech

DONG-JIN LEE

Yonsei University

Shaftesbury Road, Cambridge CB2 8EA, United Kingdom

One Liberty Plaza, 20th Floor, New York, NY 10006, USA

477 Williamstown Road, Port Melbourne, VIC 3207, Australia

314–321, 3rd Floor, Plot 3, Splendor Forum, Jasola District Centre, New Delhi – 110025, India

103 Penang Road, #05–06/07, Visioncrest Commercial, Singapore 238467

Cambridge University Press is part of Cambridge University Press & Assessment, a department of the University of Cambridge.

We share the University's mission to contribute to society through the pursuit of education, learning and research at the highest international levels of excellence.

www.cambridge.org
Information on this title: www.cambridge.org/9781009281799

DOI: 10.1017/9781009281782

First published 2023

A catalogue record for this publication is available from the British Library.

Library of Congress Cataloging-in-Publication Data
NAMES: Sirgy, M. Joseph, author. | Lee, Dong-Jin, 1962– author.
TITLE: Work-life balance : hr training for employee personal interventions /
Dr M. Joseph Sirgy, Virginia Tech. Dr Dong-Jin Lee, Yonsei University.
DESCRIPTION: New York, NY : Cambridge University Press, 2023. |
Includes bibliographical references and index.
IDENTIFIERS: LCCN 2022038902 | ISBN 9781009281799 (hardback) |
ISBN 9781009281782 (ebook)
SUBJECTS: LCSH: Work-life balance. | Personnel management. |
Employees – Training of. | Organizational learning.
CLASSIFICATION: LCC HD4904.25 .S477 2023 | DDC 650.1–dc23/eng/20220826
LC record available at https://lccn.loc.gov/2022038902

ISBN 978-1-009-28179-9 Hardback
ISBN 978-1-009-28182-9 Paperback

Contents

v

Figures

Tables

PART I

Making the Case for Work-Life Balance

In Chapter 1, we make the case for work-life balance. We do this by discussing trends in demographics, attitudes toward gender equality, and cultural norms that have set the foundation for the work-life balance movement. We introduce definitions of work-life balance accepted by the majority of scholars working in this area.

In Chapter 2, we discuss the benefits of work-life balance. Specifically, we describe the research regarding positive work-related outcomes, positive nonwork-related outcomes, and stress-related outcomes.

In Chapter 3, we discuss how work-life balance plays a major role in employee life satisfaction. Specifically, we describe the research that links work-life balance with overall life satisfaction. In doing so we discuss the principles of satisfaction in multiple domains, positive spillover of domain satisfaction, and minimal role conflict. Next, we describe how work-life balance contributes to domain satisfaction (satisfaction with work life, family life, social life, financial life, leisure life, health and safety, etc.). We also address the association between work-life balance and stress-related outcomes (emotional exhaustion, psychological distress, and mental health).

CHAPTER I

Introduction

I.I Introduction

Balance between work and family life has been a concern for employees and employers for many years, particularly over the last several decades. Many workers are attracted to "family-friendly firms." Work-life balance used to be a matter of private negotiation between employees and their employers. No more! Most employees, now more than ever, believe that they have a right to take time off around childbirth. Work-life balance programs established by many firms reflect this growing sentiment among both women and men. In recent years, the government has played a greater role in promoting employment practices that support working parents. Why?

The trend toward adopting work-life balance policies and programs may be due to greater participation of women in the workforce, which in turn may have been influenced by:

- later marriage and childbirth;
- rapid return to work after childbirth;
- higher educational achievement that increased their workplace credentials;
- increased availability of jobs that provide flexibility in scheduling and places to work from;
- the growth of the service sector (traditionally female-dominated employment opportunities) and the decline of the manufacturing sector (traditionally male-dominated employment opportunities); and
- changing norms related to greater gender equality in the workplace.

The increased proportion of women in the workforce has created pressure for work-life balance policies and programs because women often have more domestic and caretaking responsibilities than men. As such, to attract female employees and retain them, employers frequently feel obligated to develop policies and programs to make their workplace friendlier for women (Kodz, Harper, & Dench, 2002).

Furthermore, there has been a cultural shift among men who are becoming more involved in their children's upbringing, compounded by the fact that more men are assuming more responsibilities in domestic affairs given that their wives and partners are also working (Kodz, Harper, & Dench, 2002).

Another factor that has increased pressure on employers to develop and implement work-life policies and programs is the growing size of the senior population. People now live longer than ever. Who takes care of them in their old age? Their children who are adults participating in the workforce, particularly women. These workers are referred to as the "sandwich generation" – sandwiched between taking care of their own children as well as their parents. These employees demand policies and programs that accommodate their family responsibilities – childcare and elderly care (Kodz, Harper, & Dench, 2002).

Employers have also felt pressure to introduce work-life balance policies and programs in their workplace not only because of the demographic shift among employees but also because of changes in national policies. For example, many countries have developed laws related to maternity and paternity leave. Many European countries have also instituted laws related to the maximum number of hours employees have to work per week (e.g., thirty-five hours in France). Such laws have raised employers' awareness about the need to help their employees achieve work-life balance (Kodz, Harper, & Dench, 2002).

Collectively, these factors have produced a shift in cultural norms related to work-life balance policies and programs. Consider the 2000 Work-Life Balance Survey conducted by the Institute for Employment Studies in Great Britain (Kodz, Harper, & Dench, 2002). The survey results are shown in Table 1.1. The survey covered a sample of managers (employers) and workers (employees). The results clearly show that both employers' and employees' attitudes toward work-life balance policies and programs are very positive and seem to reflect the cultural norm in developed countries.

1.2   Definitions of Work-Life Balance

Work-life balance is defined in different ways. We categorize the definitions into five groups or concepts: (1) equal engagement and satisfaction in work and nonwork domains, (2) engagement in work and nonwork roles compatible with life goals, (3) successful accomplishment of goals in work and nonwork domains, (4) full engagement in multiple life domains, and

Table 1.1 *The 2000 Work-Life Balance Survey conducted in Great Britain*

Survey item	Employers (% who strongly agree or agree)	Employees (% who strongly agree or agree)
Everyone should be able to balance their work and home lives	62	81
It is not our [the employer's] responsibility to help people balance their work with other aspects of their lives	24	36
People work best when they can balance their work and other aspects of their lives	91	96

Source: Adapted from Kodz, Harper, and Dench (2002, p. 21)

(5) minimal role conflict between work and nonwork life domains. Let's discuss these definitions in some detail.

1.2.1 Equal Engagement and Satisfaction in Work and Nonwork Domains

Below are selected definitions of this first concept by notable scholars who have well-established academic credentials in work-life balance research. Greenhaus, Collins, and Shaw (2003) defined work-life balance as the extent to which individuals are equally engaged and satisfied with work and nonwork roles. That is, work-life balance is viewed in terms of an individual's perceptions of the degree of balance between time, involvement, and satisfaction pertaining to both work and nonwork roles. Clark (2000) focused on individual satisfaction and defined work-life balance as satisfaction and effective functioning at work and at home with a minimum amount of role conflict. Kirchmeyer (2000) defined work-life balance as achieving satisfying experiences in all life domains with personal resources such as energy, time, and commitment well distributed across domains. Note that all of these definitions focus on equal engagement and satisfaction across life domains. As such, individuals characterized as having work-life balance experience equal engagement and satisfaction with work and nonwork domains. They are equally involved in work and nonwork domains and obtain satisfaction from both (Clark, 2000; Greenhaus, Collins, & Shaw, 2003; Kirchmeyer, 2000).

To bring this definition to life, let's focus on how work-life balance researchers measure work-life balance based on this definition. Example survey items include:

- "Currently, I have a good balance between time I spend at work and the time I have available for nonwork activities";
- "I am satisfied with the balance between my work and private life";
- "Currently, I have a good balance between time I spend at work and the time I have available for nonwork activities."

The response scale involves a five-point Likert-type scale varying from "strongly disagree" to "strongly agree" (Brough et al., 2014).

Let's apply this definition to a person, Tom, to further illustrate. There are a total of 168 hours in a week. Tom spends approximately eleven hours a day (during the work week) engaged in work-related activities (including commuting from home to his workplace and back) – fifty-five to fifty-six hours a week in total. He is fully committed to his job and experiences a high level of job satisfaction. Furthermore, he spends another roughly fifty-five to fifty-six hours resting, sleeping, and taking care of his health and personal hygiene. This leaves roughly fifty-five to fifty-six hours that are spent in other nonwork roles such as family and social life. He feels fully committed and satisfied in his family and social roles. The time allotted to personal care, work, and nonwork is roughly the same. Tom has work-life balance.

1.2.2   Engagement in Work and Nonwork Roles Compatible with Life Goals

This category of definitions focuses on engagement in work and nonwork roles that are compatible with life values and priorities. Greenhaus and Allen (2006) have defined work-life balance as the extent to which an individual's effectiveness and satisfaction in work and family roles are compatible with the individual's life role priorities at a given point in time. Fereday and Oster (2010) viewed work-life balance as management of the actual and desired proportion of one's work and private-life activities. Thus, work-life balance allows people to achieve what they regard as most important. These definitions establish work-life balance as activities compatible with life values and priorities. Here the meaning of balance is *not* an equal level of engagement and satisfaction across life domains. It means engagement and satisfaction that is compatible with life priorities (Fereday & Oster, 2010; Greenhaus & Allen 2006, 2011; Greenhaus, Collins, & Shaw 2003).

Examples of survey measures work-life balance researchers have used to capture this construct include "How well do your work life and your family life fit together" (Valcour, 2007) and "How well do your working hours fit in with your family and social commitment." The response scale involves a five-point rating scale with the following response categories: "1 = very poorly," "2 = poorly," "3 = in-between," "4 = well," and "5= very well" (Lunau et al., 2014).

To illustrate this definition, let's consider Samantha. She has a family with two young children. Doing her best to raise her children and ensure their future happiness is the most important goal in her life. As such, she is working part time to allow her to spend more time taking care of her family. She feels that she is better equipped, both physically and mentally, to take care of her kids and maintain an effectively functioning household than her husband by spending less time at work and more time at home. Doing so is compatible with her life priorities and goals. As such, Samantha can be characterized as having a high degree of work-life balance.

1.2.3   *Successful Accomplishment of Goals in Work and Nonwork Domains*

This group of work-life balance definitions focuses on the successful accomplishment of goals in work and nonwork domains. For example, Grzywacz and Carlson (2007) asserted that work-life balance is experienced when the individual is not only fully engaged in work and nonwork roles but also successfully meeting their role-related expectations. Voydanoff (2005) defined work-life balance as a global assessment that work and family resources are sufficient to meet work and family demands such that participation is effective in both domains. Similarly, Parkes and Langford (2008) defined work-life balance as an individual's ability to meet work and family commitments as well as other nonwork responsibilities and activities. Valcour (2007) defined work-life balance as an overall level of contentment resulting from an assessment of one's degree of success at meeting work and family role demands. The common thread of these definitions is the successful performance of role expectations in work and nonwork domains. Individuals with work-life balance are fully engaged in work and nonwork domains and are successful in meeting role demands (Grzywacz & Carlson, 2007; Parkes & Langford, 2008; Valcour, 2007; Voydanoff, 2005).

Example survey items commonly used to capture work-life balance based on this definition include "It is difficult for me to balance my work and my private life" (reverse coded) and "I am meeting the requirements of both my work and my private life." The response scale involves a five-point Likert-type scale varying from "1 = strongly disagree" to "5 = strongly agree" (Syrek et al., 2011).

To bring this definition to life, let's consider the example of Pamela: she is a business executive, senior vice president of marketing, in a hospital system that spans an entire state in the United States. She is also married with three children, ages 10 through 18. Her job is taxing in that she has high-level marketing goals to meet on a quarterly basis. An example of one job-related objective is to achieve an average of 90 percent in patient satisfaction ratings across all hospitals affiliated with her healthcare company. This means that she has to implement policies and programs to ensure patient satisfaction (as captured by a patient survey). The good news is that over the last three quarters, the survey results indicate an average of 93 percent patient satisfaction. That is, Pamela has been meeting her work-related objectives. The company chief executive officer has recognized her accomplishment through not only a significant end-of-year bonus, but also a job-merit award that is widely publicized within the overall healthcare system. In addition to success at work, she is equally successful in her home life. Her kids are excelling academically. Her oldest is graduating from high school and has been accepted at a prestigious university. All three kids have a happy disposition with no problems to speak of. Her husband is very loving and is equally successful in his job. The family has taken a recent cruise in the Mediterranean, and everyone seems to have thoroughly enjoyed the trip. In other words, Pamela seems to have been equally successful in her role as a mother and wife. Pamela has work-life balance.

1.2.4   Full Engagement in Multiple Life Domains

The focus here is on full engagement in each of the roles that the person has assumed. That is, work-life balance is achieved when people are fully committed in their various social roles in work and nonwork life. In other words, work-life balance is characterized as the tendency to become fully engaged in the performance of every role in one's total role system and to approach each role with an attitude of attentiveness and care (Marks, 1977; Marks & MacDermid, 1996; Sieber, 1974). Kirchmeyer (2000) defined work-life balance as engagement in multiple roles with an approximately equal level of attention, time, involvement, and commitment. This approach to the conceptualization of work-life balance focuses on balanced engagement across the totality of roles as embedded in work and nonwork domains. That is, engagement levels are positively balanced. They are actively and fully involved in social roles in multiple life domains and have an equally high level of positive balance (Kirchmeyer, 2000; Marks, 1977; Marks & MacDermid, 1996; Sieber, 1974).

Here is an example of survey items designed to capture work-life balance from this perspective: "Due to all pressure at work, when I come home, I am often too stressed to do the things I enjoy," measured using five-point Likert scale (reverse coded); and "How often do you feel too tired after work to enjoy the things you would like to do at home" – the response scale involves a four-point rating scale with the following response categories: "1 = never," "2 = hardly ever," "3 = sometimes," and "4 = often/always" (Matthews, Bulger, & Barnes-Farrell, 2010; Sieber, 1974).

Consider the example of Anna. She juggles many roles. She is a nurse, a mother of a 7-year-old son, the wife of a physician, a caretaker of an ailing father, and primarily in charge of all household responsibilities (shopping, cooking, household bills, etc.). She fully engages in and handles these multiple roles effectively. In other words, no one is complaining that she falls short while handling her responsibilities and carrying out these many roles. The doctor she works for is happy with her work. Her son has a happy disposition and seems to be doing well at school based on his grades and the last teacher conference. Her marriage is happy and her husband often compliments her on being a "superwoman" who does a great job juggling everything. Her ailing father is equally appreciative of how she's been taking care of him. As such, Anna has a balanced life because she fully engages in multiple roles and has effectively managed all of her social roles in work and nonwork domains. Anna rates highly on work-life balance.

1.2.5 *Minimal Role Conflict between Work and Nonwork Domains*

In this category of definitions, work-life balance is defined in terms of minimal role conflict. In other words, individuals with work-life balance tend to experience minimal role conflict between work and nonwork life domains. Here, the focus of work-life balance is on the management of role conflict across life domains. As such, work-life balance is treated as satisfaction and good functioning in work and family roles with minimum role conflict (Allen et al., 2000; Clark, 2000; Kossek & Ozeki, 1998). Work-life balance is also viewed as a high degree of role enrichment with a low degree of role conflict in work and nonwork life domains (Frone, 2003; Greenhaus & Powell, 2006). That is, work-life balance is achieved through the effective management of role conflict (interference) when resources to meet role demand are threatened or lost (Fisher, Bulger, & Smith, 2009; Hobfoll, 1989). These individuals do not experience work-to-family or family-to-work role conflict. That is, they manage role conflict well (Allen et al., 2000; Clark, 2000; Fisher, Bulger, & Smith, 2009; Frone, 2003; Greenhaus & Powell, 2006; Kossek & Ozeki, 1998).

Here are examples of survey items: "I often neglect my personal needs because of the demands of my work" and "My work suffers because of everything going on in my personal life." Responses are captured using a five-point rating scale: "1 = not at all," "2 = rarely," "3 = sometimes," "4 = often," and "5 = almost all the time" (Fisher, Bulger, & Smith, 2009).

Let's consider the case of George. George works in the IT department of a university. The department is short-staffed. The workload at the beginning of each semester is immense, to the point that he has to leave work, get a reprieve of a couple of hours for dinner, and go back to work for another three–four hours before he conks out from fatigue. George went along with this arrangement mostly because his boss has been signing bonus checks for the extra time George has been working. However, George has a girlfriend who has been complaining about the fact that he does not "have a life." It is obvious in this situation that George is experiencing role conflict – major conflict between his work life and love life. What to do? He needs to minimize role conflict; otherwise, he is very likely to lose his girlfriend. In other words, he needs to achieve a semblance of work-life balance by minimizing the conflict between his IT role and his boyfriend role. He starts looking for other IT jobs in organizations where work demand seems stable over time. He finds one in a neighboring hospital. Perfect! The interview went well and the hospital administration made him a job offer. The offer amounts to a parallel move – that is, there is no increase in responsibility or money. He is not enamored with the job offer, and he still likes the people he is working with at the university. He even likes his boss. Armed with that offer, he talks to his supervisor and pleads his case. He makes it clear to his boss that he cannot work after hours irrespective of the workload. Although he does not threaten to quit, he drops a hint that if push comes to shove, he will seriously consider jumping ship. His boss expresses sympathy and finally caves in; his boss reduced his workload, which allowed him to "have a life" after the official work hours. George has finally achieved work-life balance.

1.3 Conclusion

In this chapter we have discussed trends in population demographics, changing attitudes about gender equity in the workplace, and national legislation as factors increasing pressure on employers to offer work-life balance initiatives to stay competitive and abide by the law. We introduced the reader to five different definitions and subjective measures of work-life balance. The key characteristics of these definitions are: (1) equal engagement and satisfaction in work and nonwork domains, (2) engagement in work and nonwork roles compatible with life goals, (3) successful accomplishment of goals in work and nonwork domains, (4) full engagement in multiple life domains, and (5) minimal role conflict between work and nonwork domains (see Table 1.2 for a summary). These definitions focus on various ways of effective role engagement (equal, goal-reflected, and full engagement) as well as the results of such effective engagement (i.e., successful accomplishment of goals and minimal role conflict). As one can see, the concept of work-life balance can be viewed from different perspectives resulting in different definitions based on these perspectives. Having said this, there is a common thread running through these different definitions, namely engagement in both work and nonwork roles in ways to meet role demand and minimize role conflict. This is the ultimate definition of work-life balance that we would like to impress upon the reader. Let's keep this definition in mind as you read the subsequent chapters.

It is important for organizations to measure work-life balance both subjectively and objectively. We provided the reader with several definitions of work-life balance and examples of survey measures. These are obviously "subjective indicators" of work-life balance. Objective indicators are more elusive. One can capture this construct through several indicators that would involve a composite index. Work-life balance in organizations in specific industries or sectors can be captured through a survey targeting the human resource (HR) directors in which the directors are asked to report the following:

- *Workload* – employees' average actual hours spent at work, frequency of employees' overtime or night time work, and employees' proportion of time spent at work (Kossek, Valcour, & Lirio, 2014);
- *Flexible work schedules* – availability of a program that allows employees flexibility in terms of work times, the extent to which employees have a choice in selecting their own work schedule, the extent of actual program use, and the availability of financial support for such a program (Baltes et al., 1999);
- *Flexible workplace* – availability of a program that allows flexibility of workplaces, the extent to which employees have a choice in selecting places where they can work, the extent of actual program use, and the availability of financial support for such a program (Kossek, Lautsch, & Eaton, 2006; McCarthy, Darcy, & Grady, 2010);

Table 1.2 *Definitions and key characteristics of work-life balance*

Key characteristics	Definitions with key characteristics	References
Equal engagement and satisfaction in work and nonwork domains	Work-life balance is defined as the extent to which individuals are equally engaged and satisfied with work and nonwork roles.	Greenhaus, Collins, and Shaw (2003)
	Engagement in work and nonwork roles to produce equal amounts of satisfaction in work and nonwork life domains.	Clark (2000); Kirchmeyer (2000)
	Individuals characterized as high on work-life balance devote their time and psychological energy in balanced ways while deriving much satisfaction from nonwork life domains.	Greenhaus, Collins, and Shaw (2003)
Engagement in work and nonwork roles compatible with life goals	Work-life balance is viewed as an individual's effectiveness and satisfaction in work and nonwork roles being compatible with the individual's values and priorities.	Greenhaus and Allen (2006)
	Work-life balance is defined as an overall appraisal of the extent to which the individual's effectiveness and satisfaction in work and family roles are consistent with their life values at a given point in time.	Greenhaus and Allen (2011)
	Work-life balance is the management of the actual and desired proportion of one's work and private-life activities.	Fereday and Oster (2010)
Successful accomplishment of goals in work and nonwork domains	Work-life balance is experienced when the individual is fully engaged in the roles in various life domains and successfully accomplishing these role-related expectations.	Grzywacz and Carlson (2007)
	A global assessment that work and family resources are sufficient to meet work and family demands such that participation is effective in both domains.	Voydanoff (2005)
	An individual's ability to meet work and family commitments as well as other nonwork responsibilities and activities.	Parkes and Langford (2008)
	An overall level of contentment resulting from an assessment of one's degree of success at meeting work and family role demands.	Valcour (2007)

Table 1.2 (*cont.*)

Key characteristics	Definitions with key characteristics	References
Full engagement in multiple life domains	The tendency to become fully engaged in the performance of every role in one's total role system to approach each role and role partner with an attitude of attentiveness and care.	Marks (1977); Marks and MacDermid (1996); Sieber (1974)
	Engagement in multiple roles with an approximately equal level of attention, time, involvement, or commitment	Kirchmeyer (2000)
Minimal role conflict between work and nonwork domains	Satisfaction and good functioning in work and family roles with minimum role conflict.	Allen et al. (2000); Clark (2000); Kossek and Ozeki (1998)
	A high degree of role enrichment with a low degree of role conflict in work and nonwork life domains.	Frone (2003); Greenhaus and Powell (2006)
	Work-life balance is achieved through effective management of role conflict (interference) when resources to meet role demand are threatened or lost.	Fisher, Bulger, and Smith (2009); Hobfoll (1989)

- *Family care* – availability of a child/elderly care program that allows employees to place their children or elderly parents in a care facility while the employees are working; the extent to which employees have a choice in selecting a preferred care facility, the extent of actual program use, and the availability of financial support for such a program (McCarthy, Darcy, & Grady, 2010); and
- *Job sharing* – availability of a program that allows two or more employees to share one job position, the extent to which employees have a choice in selecting the job position to be shared; the extent of actual program use, and the availability of financial support for such a program (Allen, 2001; Galinsky, Bond, & Friedman, 1993).

Work-life balance is freely determined by the individual but is facilitated and constrained by a wide range of factors operating at a micro (individual), meso (organizational), and macro (national) level (Gregory & Milner, 2009). For example, individual choice in managing work-life balance is constrained by organizational culture, which in turn is strongly related to its sector-specific culture.

This book will evaluate and discuss when work-life programs are effective by examining individual interventions for work-life balance. Simply offering family-friendly benefits is insufficient. It is necessary to train employees to use their own resources (intellectual, emotional, and social) to achieve work-life balance on their own. This book reviews and provides practical guidelines for personal interventions for work-life balance.

References

Allen, T. D. (2001). Family-supportive work environments: The role of organizational perceptions. *Journal of Vocational Behavior*, 58(3), 414–435.

Allen, T. D., Herst, D. E., Bruck, C. S., & Sutton, M. (2000). Consequences associated with work-to-family conflict: A review and agenda for future research. *Journal of Occupational Health Psychology*, 5(2), 278–308.

Baltes, B. B., Briggs, T. E., Huff, J. W., Wright, J. A., & Neuman, G. A. (1999). Flexible and compressed workweek schedules: A meta-analysis of their effects on work-related criteria. *Journal of Applied Psychology*, 84(4), 496–513.

Brough, P., Timms, C., O'Driscoll, M. P. et al. (2014). Work-life balance: A longitudinal evaluation of a new measure across Australia and New Zealand workers. *International Journal of Human Resource Management*, 25(19), 2724–2744.

Clark, S. C. (2000). Work/family border theory: A new theory of work/family balance. *Human Relations*, 53(6), 747–770.

Fereday, J. & Oster, C. (2010). Managing a work-life balance: The experiences of midwives working in a group practice setting. *Midwifery*, 26(3), 311–318.

Fisher, G. G., Bulger, C. A., & Smith, C. S. (2009). Beyond work and family: A measure of work/nonwork interference and enhancement. *Journal of Occupational Health Psychology*, 14(4), 441–456.

Frone, M. R. (2003). Work-family balance. In J. C. Quick & L. E. Tetrick (Eds.), *Handbook of occupational health psychology* (pp. 143–162). Washington, DC: American Psychological Association.

Galinsky, E., Bond, J. T., & Friedman, D. E. (1993). *The changing workforce: Highlights of the national study*. Darby, PA: Diane Publishing.

Greenhaus, J. H. & Allen, T. D. (2006). Work-family balance: Exploration of a concept. Paper presented at the Families and Work Conference, Provo, UT.

Greenhaus, J. H. & Allen, T. D. (2011). Work-family balance: A review and extension of the literature. In J. C. Quick & L. E. Tetrick (Eds.), *Handbook of occupational health psychology* (pp. 165–183). Washington, DC: American Psychological Association.

Greenhaus, J. H. & Powell, G. N. (2006). When work and family are allies: A theory of work-family enrichment. *Academy of Management Review*, 31(1), 72–92.

Greenhaus, J. H., Collins, K. M., & Shaw, J. D. (2003). The relation between work-family balance and quality of life. *Journal of Vocational Behavior*, 63(3), 510–531.

Gregory, A. & Milner, S. E. (2009). Work-life balance: A matter of choice? *Gender, Work and Organization*, 16(1), 1–13.

Grzywacz, J. G. & Carlson, D. S. (2007). Conceptualizing work-family balance: Implications for practice and research. *Advances in Developing Human Resources*, 9(4), 455–471.

Hobfoll, S. E. (1989). Conservation of resources: A new attempt at conceptualizing stress. *American Psychologist*, 44(3), 513–525.

Kirchmeyer, C. (2000). Work-life initiatives: Greed or benevolence regarding workers' time? In C. L. Cooper & D. M. Rousseau (Eds.), *Trends in organizational behavior, Vol. 7. Time in organizational behavior* (pp. 79–93). New York: John Wiley & Sons.

Kodz, J., Harper, H., & Dench, S. (2002). *Work-life balance: Beyond the rhetoric.* Brighton, UK: Institute for Employment Studies.

Kossek, E. E. & Ozeki, C. (1998). Work-family conflict, policies, and the job–life satisfaction relationship: A review and directions for organizational behavior–human resources research. *Journal of Applied Psychology*, 83(2), 139–155.

Kossek, E. E., Lautsch, B. A., & Eaton, S. C. (2006). Telecommuting, control, and boundary management: Correlates of policy use and practice, job control, and work-family effectiveness. *Journal of Vocational Behavior*, 68(2), 347–367.

Kossek, E. E., Valcour, M., & Lirio, P. (2014). Organizational strategies for promoting work-life balance and wellbeing. In Y. Peter & C. L. Cooper (Eds.), *Work and wellbeing: A Complete Reference Guide* (pp. 295–318). New York: John Wiley & Sons.

Lunau, T., Bambra, C., Eikemo, T. A., van Der Wel, K. A., & Dragano, N. (2014). A balancing act? Work-life balance, health and well-being in European welfare states. *European Journal of Public Health*, 24(3), 422–427.

Marks, S. R. (1977). Multiple roles and strain: Some notes on human energy, time and commitment. *American Sociological Review*, 42(6), 921–936.

Marks, S. R. & MacDermid, S. M. (1996). Multiple roles and the self: A theory of role balance. *Journal of Marriage and the Family*, 58(2), 417–432.

Matthews, R. A., Bulger, C. A., & Barnes-Farrell, J. L. (2010). Work social supports, role stressors, and work-family conflict: The moderating effect of age. *Journal of Vocational Behavior*, 76(1), 78–90.

McCarthy, A., Darcy, C., & Grady, G. (2010). Work-life balance policy and practice: Understanding line manager attitudes and behaviors. *Human Resource Management Review*, 20(2), 158–167.

Parkes, L. P. & Langford, P. H. (2008). Work-life balance or work-life alignment? A test of the importance of work-life balance for employee engagement and intention to stay in organisations. *Journal of Management & Organization*, 14(3), 267–284.

Sieber, S. D. (1974). Toward a theory of role accumulation. *American Sociological Review*, 39(4), 567–578.

Syrek, C., Bauer-Emmel, C., Antoni, C., & Klusemann, J. (2011). Entwicklung und validierung der trierer kurzskala zur messung von work-life balance (TKS-WLB). *Diagnostica*, July 5.

Valcour, M. (2007). Work-based resources as moderators of the relationship between work hours and satisfaction with work-family balance. *Journal of Applied Psychology*, 92(6), 1512–1523.

Voydanoff, P. (2005). Consequences of boundary-spanning demands and resources for work-to-family conflict and perceived stress. *Journal of Occupational Health Psychology*, 10(4), 491–503.

CHAPTER 2

Why is Work-Life Balance Important?

2.1 Introduction

Consider the following statistics (https://comparecamp.com/work-life-balance-statistics/):

- 65 percent of employees report that workplace stress has caused various difficulties in their lives; and additionally, about 10 percent say that workplace stress has caused major issues in their personal lives;
- 62 percent of workers feel neck pain at the end of the day due to stress;
- More than 50 percent of respondents report that they often skip lunch due to their heavy workload;
- Around 34 percent report difficulty in sleeping due to ongoing work-related stress;
- Up to 44 percent of employees report eye strain;
- Due to various physical issues stemming from job stress, around 12 percent had called in sick and missed work;
- Around 27 percent of workers report being depressed due to their workload;
- Companies that offer better work-life balance have a 25 percent lower employee turnover;
- 24 percent of employees who enjoy some form of a work-life balance program, such as working from home at least once a month, are significantly happier and more productive;
- 85 percent of businesses that provide work-life balance opportunities report that they are more productive;
- A Stanford University study showed that work-life balance programs, such as remote working, could lead to a 13 percent performance increase;

- 33 percent of employees who enjoy work-life balance benefits plan to stay in their current companies;
- Around 21 percent of workers with good work-life balance tend to work harder;
- Companies with employees who benefit from a good work-life balance report that their healthcare expenditure is 50 percent lower; and
- Happy employees are less likely to be absent, which saves businesses about $2,600 per employee.

These statistics hint at the fact that work-life balance programs are highly beneficial for employers and employees alike. Discussed below is a much more systematic analysis of the benefits of work-life balance intervention programs based on well-established science.

2.2   Benefits of Work-Life Balance Programs

Significant research has empirically demonstrated that work-life balance produces positive work-related, nonwork related, and stress-related outcomes (see Sirgy & Lee, 2018 for review). See Figure 2.1.

2.2.1   *Positive Work-Related Outcomes*

Work-life balance produces many positive work-related outcomes. Research has found that work-life balance of employees increases job performance, job satisfaction, organizational commitment, career development, and success. Research has also demonstrated that work-life balance reduces job malfunction, job burnout and alienation, absenteeism, and turnover intention. Specifically, as work-life balance increases,

- job performance increases (e.g., Blazovich, Smith, & Smith, 2014; Carlson, Grzywacz, & Kacmar, 2010; Frone, Yardley, & Markel, 1997; Wayne, Musisca, & Fleeson, 2004; Whiston & Cinamon, 2015);
- job satisfaction increases (e.g., Allen et al., 2000; Anaton, 2013; Carlson et al., 2006; De Simone et al., 2014; Fisher, Bulger, & Smith, 2009; Kossek & Ozeki, 1998; Whiston & Cinamon, 2015);
- job malfunction decreases (e.g., Whiston & Cinamon, 2015),
- career development is enhanced (e.g., Konrad & Yang, 2012; Whiston & Cinamon, 2015);
- perceptions of subjective career success are heightened (e.g., Allen et al., 2000; Kossek & Ozeki, 1998);

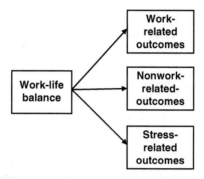

Figure 2.1   Consequences of work-life balance

- organizational commitment increases (e.g., Allen et al., 2000; Kossek & Ozeki, 1998),
- intentions to leave the organization diminish (e.g., Allen et al., 2000; Kossek & Ozeki, 1998; McNall, Masuda, & Nicklin, 2010);
- absenteeism decreases (e.g., Frone, Yardley, & Markel, 1997; Wayne, Musisca, & Fleeson, 2004); and
- turnover decreases (e.g., Frone, Yardley, & Markel, 1997; Wayne, Musisca, & Fleeson, 2004).

2.2.2   Positive Nonwork-Related Outcomes

Work-life balance has positive nonwork outcomes as well. Research has shown that work-life balance of employees increases employees' life satisfaction, marital satisfaction, family performance, family satisfaction, parental satisfaction, and leisure satisfaction. Research also found that work-life balance of employees reduces health conditions, cognitive problems, and conflicts with family members. Specifically, much of the research has shown that as work-life balance increases,

- life satisfaction increases (e.g., Allen et al., 2000; Anaton, 2013; Carlson et al., 2006; De Simone et al., 2014; Fisher, Bulger, & Smith, 2009; Greenhaus & Beutell, 1985; Kossek & Ozeki, 1998; Schaufeli et al., 2002; Schaufeli & Bakker, 2004);
- marital adjustment and satisfaction are heightened (e.g., Allen et al., 2000; Kossek & Ozeki, 1998; Whiston & Cinamon, 2015),
- family performance improves (e.g., Allen et al., 2000; Carlson, Grzywacz, & Kacmar, 2010; Kossek & Ozeki, 1998);

- family satisfaction increases (e.g., Allen et al., 2000; Carlson et al., 2006; Fisher, Bulger, & Smith, 2009; Kossek & Ozeki, 1998; Whiston & Cinamon, 2015);
- parental satisfaction increases (e.g., Allen et al., 2000; Kossek & Ozeki, 1998);
- satisfaction with leisure activities increases (e.g., Allen et al., 2000; Kossek & Ozeki, 1998); and
- conflict with other family members diminishes (e.g., Westman & Etzion, 2005).

2.2.3 Stress-Related Outcomes

Work-life balance reduces psychological distress. Research has shown that work-life conflict increases psychological distress (i.e., emotional exhaustion, emotional ill-being, anxiety, irritability and hostility, hypertension, and depression) and family-related stress (i.e., affective parental and marital stress), as well as detrimental physiological symptoms (i.e., somatic complaints, high blood pressure and cholesterol, alcohol abuse, and cigarette consumption). Research has also demonstrated significant links between work-life conflict and stress. Specifically, as work-life balance decreases,

- psychological distress increases (e.g., Whiston & Cinamon, 2015), and general life stress increases – being upset and frustrated, or tense (e.g., Allen et al., 2000; Frone, Russell, & Cooper, 1992; Kossek & Ozeki, 1998);
- emotional exhaustion increases (e.g., Lee & Kim, 2013);
- emotional ill-being increases (e.g., Whiston & Cinamon, 2015);
- anxiety increases (e.g., Allen et al., 2000; Frone, Russell, & Cooper, 1992; Kossek & Ozeki, 1998);
- irritability/hostility increases (e.g., Allen et al., 2000; Kossek & Ozeki, 1998);
- hypertension increases (e.g., Allen et al., 2000; Kossek & Ozeki, 1998);
- depression increases (e.g., Allen et al., 2000; Kossek & Ozeki, 1998; Whiston & Cinamon, 2015);
- family-related stress increases (e.g., Allen et al., 2000; Kossek & Ozeki, 1998);
- affective parental and marital stress increase (e.g., Allen et al., 2000; Kossek & Ozeki, 1998);
- manifestation of illness symptoms increases (e.g., Allen et al., 2000; Kossek & Ozeki, 1998);

Table 2.1 *Consequences of work-life balance*

Type	Outcome	References
Work-related outcomes	Job performance (+)	Blazovich, Smith, and Smith (2014); Carlson, Grzywacz, and Kacmar (2010); Frone, Yardley, and Markel (1997); Wayne, Musisca, and Fleeson (2004); Whiston and Cinamon (2015)
	Job satisfaction (+)	Allen et al. (2000); Anaton (2013); Carlson et al. (2006); De Simone et al. (2014); Fisher, Bulger, and Smith (2009); Kossek and Ozeki (1998); Whiston and Cinamon (2015)
	Organizational commitment (+)	Allen et al. (2000); Kossek and Ozeki (1998)
	Intentions to leave the organization (–)	Allen et al. (2000); Kossek and Ozeki (1998); McNall, Masuda, and Nicklin (2010)
	Career development (+)	Konrad and Yang (2012); Whiston and Cinamon (2015)
	Perceptions of career success (+)	Allen et al. (2000); Kossek and Ozeki (1998)
	Job malfunction (–)	Whiston and Cinamon (2015)
	Job burnout (–)	Allen et al. (2000); Frone, Yardley, and Markel (1997); Kossek and Ozeki (1998); Wayne, Musisca, and Fleeson (2004)
	Work alienation (–)	Allen et al. (2000); Kossek and Ozeki (1998)
	Absenteeism (–)	Frone, Yardley, and Markel (1997); Wayne, Musisca, and Fleeson (2004)
	Turnover intentions (–)	Frone, Yardley, and Markel (1997); Wayne, Musisca, and Fleeson (2004)
Nonwork related outcomes	Life satisfaction (+)	Allen et al. (2000); Anaton (2013); Carlson et al. (2006); De Simone et al. (2014); Fisher, Bulger, and Smith (2009); Greenhaus and Beutell (1985); Kossek and Ozeki (1998); Schaufeli et al. (2002); Schaufeli and Bakker (2004)
	Marital adjustment and marital satisfaction (+)	Allen et al. (2000); Kossek and Ozeki (1998); Whiston & Cinamon (2015)
	Family performance (+)	Allen et al. (2000); Carlson, Grzywacz, and Kacmar (2010); Kossek & Ozeki (1998)
	Family satisfaction (+)	Allen et al. (2000); Carlson et al. (2006); Fisher, Bulger, and Smith (2009); Kossek and Ozeki (1998); Whiston and Cinamon (2015)
	Parental satisfaction (+)	Allen et al. (2000); Kossek and Ozeki (1998)
	Satisfaction with leisure activities (+)	Allen et al. (2000); Kossek and Ozeki (1998)
	Conflict with other family members (–)	Westman and Erzion (2005)

Stress-related outcomes	Psychological distress (–)	Whiston and Cinamon (2015)
	General life stress (being upset and frustrated, or tense) (–)	Allen et al. (2000); Frone, Russell, and Cooper (1992); Kossek and Ozeki (1998)
	Emotional exhaustion (–)	Lee and Kim (2013)
	Emotional ill-being (–)	Whiston and Cinamon (2015)
	Anxiety (–)	Allen et al. (2000); Frone, Russell, and Cooper (1992); Kossek and Ozeki (1998)
	Irritability/hostility (–)	Allen et al. (2000); Kossek and Ozeki (1998)
	Hypertension (–)	Allen et al. (2000); Kossek and Ozeki (1998)
	Depression (–)	Allen et al. (2000); Kossek and Ozeki (1998); Whiston & Cinamon (2015)
	Family-related stress (–)	Allen et al. (2000); Kossek and Ozeki (1998)
	Affective parental and marital stress (–)	Allen et al. (2000); Kossek and Ozeki (1998)
	Manifestation of illness symptoms (–)	Allen et al. (2000); Kossek and Ozeki (1998)
	Somatic complaints (e.g., loss of appetite, fatigue, and nervous tension) (–)	Allen et al. (2000); Kossek and Ozeki (1998); Whiston & Cinamon (2015)
	Blood pressure and cholesterol (+)	Allen et al. (2000); Kossek and Ozeki (1998)
	Incidence of alcohol abuse (–)	Allen et al. (2000); Kossek and Ozeki (1998); Whiston & Cinamon (2015)
	Incidence of cigarette consumption (–)	Allen et al. (2000); Kossek and Ozeki (1998)

- somatic complaints (e.g., loss of appetite, fatigue, and nervous tension) increase (e.g., Allen et al., 2000; Kossek & Ozeki, 1998; Whiston & Cinamon, 2015);
- blood pressure and cholesterol become elevated (e.g., Allen et al., 2000; Kossek & Ozeki, 1998);
- incidence of alcohol abuse increases (e.g., Allen et al., 2000; Kossek & Ozeki, 1998; Whiston & Cinamon, 2015); and
- incidence of cigarette consumption increases (e.g., Allen et al., 2000; Kossek & Ozeki, 1998).

2.3   Conclusion

Why is work-life balance important for both employees and organizations? We made the case that work-life balance is important because compelling research has shown that work-life balance influences a host of organizational outcomes (e.g., organizational identification, loyalty, commitment, turnover, job performance, employee morale, and organizational citizenship) and personal outcomes (employee stress, employee burnout, employee wellbeing, satisfaction with life overall, personal happiness, psychological wellbeing or eudaimonia, satisfaction with family life, satisfaction with social life, satisfaction with leisure life, satisfaction with spiritual life, satisfaction with financial life, etc.). See Table 2.1 for a summary of this discussion.

It should be noted that many of the outcomes (work, nonwork, and stress-related outcomes) are interrelated. For example, role conflict increases psychological distress, which reduces job satisfaction and family life satisfaction. In addition, psychological distress can cause health problems and unhealthy consumption behaviors (Frone, 2003).

References

Allen, T. D., Herst, D. E., Bruck, C. S., & Sutton, M. (2000). Consequences associated with work-to-family conflict: A review and agenda for future research. *Journal of Occupational Health Psychology*, 5(2), 278–308.

Anaton, L. (2013). A proposed conceptual framework of work-family/family-work facilitation (WFF/FWF) approach in inter-role conflict. *Journal of Global Management*, 6(1), 89–100.

Blazovich, J. L., Smith, K. T., & Smith, L. M. (2014). Employee-friendly companies and work-life balance: Is there an impact on financial performance and risk level? *Journal of Organizational Culture, Communications and Conflict*, 18(1), 1–13.

Carlson, D. S., Grzywacz, J. G., & Kacmar, K. M. (2010). The relationship of schedule flexibility and outcomes via the work-family interface. *Journal of Managerial Psychology*, 25(4), 330–355.

Carlson, D. S., Kacmar, K. M., Wayne, J. H., & Grzywacz, J. G. (2006). Measuring the positive side of the work-family work/family interface: Development and validation of a work-family enrichment scale. *Journal of Vocational Behavior*, 68(1), 131–164.

De Simone, S., Lampis, J., & Lasio, D. et al. (2014). Influences of work-family interface on job and life satisfaction. *Applied Research in Quality of Life*, 9(4), 831–861.

Fisher, G. G., Bulger, C. A., & Smith, C. S. (2009). Beyond work and family: a measure of work/nonwork interference and enhancement. *Journal of Occupational Health Psychology*, 14(4), 441–456.

Frone, M. R. (2003). Work-family balance. In J. C. Quick & L. E. Tetrick (Eds.), *Handbook of occupational health psychology* (pp. 143–162). Washington, DC: American Psychological Association.

Frone, M. R., Russell, M., & Cooper, M. L. (1992). Antecedents and outcomes of work-family conflict: Testing a model of the work-family interface. *Journal of Applied Psychology*, 77(1), 65–78.

Frone, M. R., Yardley, J. K., & Markel, K. S. (1997). Developing and testing an integrative model of the work-family interface. *Journal of Vocational Behavior*, 50(2), 145–167.

Greenhaus, J. H. & Beutell, N. J. (1985). Sources of conflict between work and family roles. *Academy of Management Review*, 10(1), 76–88.

Konrad, A. M. & Yang, Y. (2012). Is using work-life interface benefits a career-limiting move? An examination of women, men, lone parents, and parents with partners. *Journal of Organizational Behavior*, 33(8), 1095–1119.

Kossek, E. E. & Ozeki, C. (1998). Work-family conflict, policies, and the job-life satisfaction relationship: A review and directions for organizational behavior–human resources research. *Journal of Applied Psychology*, 83(2), 139–155.

Lee, S. & Kim, S. L. (2013). Social support, work-family conflict, and emotional exhaustion in South Korea. *Psychological Reports*, 113(2), 619–634.

McNall, L. A., Masuda, A. D., & Nicklin, J. M. (2010). Flexible work arrangements and job satisfaction/turnover intentions: The mediating role of work-to-family enrichment. *Journal of Psychology: Interdisciplinary and Applied*, 144(1), 61–81.

Schaufeli, W. B. & Bakker, A. B. (2004). Job demands, job resources and their relationship with burnout and engagement: A multi-sample study. *Journal of Organizational Behavior*, 25(3), 293–315.

Schaufeli, W. B., Salanova, M., Gonzalez-Roma, V., & Bakker, A. B. (2002). The measurement of engagement and burnout and: a confirmative analytic approach. *Journal of Happiness Studies*, 3(1), 71–92.

Sirgy, M. J. & Lee, D.-J. (2018). Work-life balance: An integrative review. *Applied Research in Quality of Life*, 13(1), 229–254.

Wayne, J. H., Musisca, N., & Fleeson, W. (2004). Considering the role of personality in the work-family experience: Relationships of the big five to work-family conflict and facilitation. *Journal of Vocational Behavior*, 64(1), 108–130.

Westman, M. & Etzion, D. (2005). The crossover of work-family conflict from one spouse to the other. *Journal of Applied Social Psychology*, 35(9), 1936–1957.

Whiston, S. C. & Cinamon, R. G. (2015). The work-family interface: Integrating research and career counselling practice. *Career Development Quarterly*, 63(1), 44–56.

CHAPTER 3

How Does Work-Life Balance
Contribute to Life Satisfaction?

3.1 Work-Life Balance and Overall Life Satisfaction

How does work-life balance contribute to overall life satisfaction? Here are several explanations that can help the reader better understand the influence of work-life balance on life satisfaction.

3.1.1 Satisfaction in Multiple Domains

Individuals with a balanced life tend to be fully engaged in multiple roles. Engaging in a single role does not significantly contribute to overall life satisfaction. When people become engaged in only one life domain (e.g., work life), they are not likely to experience overall life satisfaction because the amount of satisfaction that we can extract from a single life domain is limited. We have to keep in mind that overall life satisfaction is mostly determined by an aggregation of satisfaction from various life domains. When employees engage in multiple social roles and have satisfied the full spectrum of development needs, they are likely to experience a high level of overall life satisfaction (Sirgy & Lee, 2016). That is, when employees are fully engaged in various social roles they identify with and are successful in these roles, they are likely to have a positive self-image and enhanced subjective wellbeing (Voydanoff, 2005). In contrast, lack of active involvement and alienation in a life domain results in decreased life satisfaction.

Let's consider the case of Sam. Sam is a workaholic. He is a sales rep in a pharmaceutical company. He is very passionate about his work and believes in the efficacy of the diabetic drug he is promoting to primary care physicians in his assigned territory. He is married to his job. He is constantly on the road traveling from one clinic to another. He is successful at his job and is making plenty of money on sales commissions. But is he truly happy? Not likely! The reason, as we explained above, is that he can only extract a limited amount of satisfaction from his work life. To be genuinely happy, he must also be satisfied with his social life, his leisure life, his love life, his family life, and his spiritual life, among other important life domains. In other words, true satisfaction with life comes not only from work life; it comes from satisfaction in multiple domains. Each domain can only contribute a limited amount of satisfaction to overall life satisfaction. As such, Sam has an imbalanced life, and this imbalance detracts from his overall life satisfaction.

3.1.2   Positive Spillover of Domain Satisfaction

Employees with a balanced life are likely to experience positive spillover across life domains (Frone, 2003; Greenhaus & Powell, 2006). Positive spillover refers to positive mood, skills, values, and behaviors that transfer from one life domain to another (Edwards & Rothbard, 2000). For example, when a person has a good day at work, their good mood carries over when they come home. This is "mood positive spillover." An example of "skill positive spillover" is punctuality. A mother is punctual at work and raises her children to be punctual too. She gets them up in the morning by 7:00 a.m., prepares breakfast, and drops them off at school by no later than 8:00 a.m. She does this punctually every school day.

Greenhaus and Powell (2006) have argued that engagement in multiple roles may result in high levels of subjective wellbeing through the transfer of positive experiences from one life domain to another. Learning that occurs in one life domain is easily transferred to other life domains, thus enhancing role engagement and effectiveness in multiple domains. For example, a woman may feel that being a mother taught her patience, which served her well as a manager at work.

3.1.3   Minimal Role Conflict

Workers who have a balanced life are less likely to experience role conflict across life domains (Greenhaus & Beutell, 1985). Because workers have finite physical and psychological resources (time, attention, energy), imbalanced involvement in a particular role makes it difficult to engage in activities of a competing role (Edwards & Rothbard, 2000). For instance, when workers devote a significant portion of their time, attention, and energy to one role (e.g., work life), they are likely to experience difficulty in meeting the demands of another role (e.g., family life). In this case, they experience conflict between work life and family life. Invariably, role conflict takes a toll on life satisfaction. In contrast, employees with a balanced life typically invest only enough time and energy to be successful in their roles and thus experience minimal role conflict. They effectively manage the borders of their life domains in a manner that leads to high levels of overall life satisfaction.

3.1.4   Summary

To sum up this discussion related to how work-life balance contributes to overall life satisfaction, we made the case that the two are strongly connected. The role of work-life balance in life satisfaction involves satisfaction in multiple domains, positive spillover of domain satisfaction, and minimal role conflict (see Table 3.1). Specifically, we demonstrated that overall life satisfaction is mostly determined from *satisfaction extracted from multiple life domains*. That is, the more satisfied employees are with their life domains outside of work life, the more likely they are to also be satisfied with their life overall. By the same token, satisfaction extracted from multiple life domains increases the chances that both high- and low-order needs are met – high-order needs are growth needs (e.g., the need for self-actualization) and low-order needs are essentially basic needs (e.g., need for food and shelter). Furthermore, satisfaction extracted from multiple domains increases the likelihood of boosting self-esteem, which in turn plays an important role in life satisfaction. That is, the more satisfied employees are in work and non-work domains, the more likely that they may construe their self-concepts positively in their work and nonwork roles.

Positive spillover of domain satisfaction is the second explanation. That is, work-life balance contributes to life satisfaction through a psychological process involving positive spillover of domain satisfaction. Specifically, satisfaction in each life domain contributes to satisfaction with overall life; but it does so multiplicatively rather than additively. In other words, life satisfaction increases significantly when positive feelings in one life domain (e.g., social life, family life, leisure life) spills over to work life thus amplifying the summative satisfaction effect on overall life satisfaction. Positive spillover between life domains occurs when the employee applies skills, values, privileges, status, and emotions experienced in one life domain to another.

Finally, work-life balance contributes to life satisfaction by minimizing stress arising from *role conflict*. Balanced employees are likely to experience greater life satisfaction because they invest only enough time and energy to be successful in their roles, thus better avoiding role conflict. They do so by managing the borders of their life domains. That is, they make every attempt possible to allocate sufficient time, energy, and resources to meet not only demands from their work role but also their nonwork roles.

Table 3.1 *Work-life balance and overall life satisfaction*

Work-Life Balance Contributes to:	Individuals with Work-Life Balance Are Likely to:	References
Satisfaction in multiple domains	Obtain satisfaction from multiple life domains. Obtain satisfaction from high- and low-order needs. Experience a positive self-image from successfully meeting role demands.	Voydanoff (2005)
Positive spillover of domain satisfaction	Experience positive spillover across life domains Successfully transfer skills, values, privileges, status, and affect in a life domain into another life domain.	Greenhaus and Beutell (1985); Frone (2003); Greenhaus and Powell (2006)
Minimal role conflict	Invest only enough time and energy to be successful in their roles and avoid experiencing role conflict. Successfully manage the borders of their life domains, thus minimizing role conflict.	Greenhaus and Beutell (1985); Edwards and Rothbard (2000)

Doing so serves to minimize role conflict, thus reducing stress, which in turn helps to maintain an acceptable level of life satisfaction.

3.2   Work-Life Balance and Domain Satisfaction

Work-life balance contributes positively and significantly to domain satisfaction. Specifically, work-life balance contributes to satisfaction in marital life, family life, health and safety, and leisure life.

3.2.1   Satisfaction with Marital Life

Work-life balance increases satisfaction in *marital life*. Balanced workers are likely to have a reduced workload that allows them to engage fully in family roles resulting in reduced work-family conflict. They are also likely to experience increased control over when and where they work, which also serves to reduce work-to-family conflict (work interfering with family life) and family-to-work conflict (family life interfering with work)

(Allen et al., 2000; Kossek & Ozeki, 1998). Furthermore, workers with a balanced life are likely to exert better control over their work schedule (e.g., flextime) and place of work (e.g., telecommuting). As such, they are able to better handle the demand of their family role, which in turn serves to reduce work-family conflict. Research has shown that work-life conflict is negatively associated with marital adjustment (Greenhaus et al., 1987; Parasuraman et al., 1989).

For example, consider the case of David. David works at a company that allows him to work from home (place flexibility). Doing so allows him to do a better job attending to his family needs – doing house chores and taking charge of the kids' homework. The result is that his wife, Deborah, is happy with him and he feels it (marital satisfaction).

3.2.2 Satisfaction with Family Life

Work-life balance serves to increase satisfaction in *family life*. Individuals with high work-life balance are likely to have more time for family activities. They can meet the demand of their family roles, thereby increasing family life satisfaction (Brough et al., 2014; Frone, 2003; Johnson, Zabriskie, & Hill, 2006; Westman & Etzion, 2005). The same individuals are also likely to experience a low degree of work-life conflict. Research has found that work-life conflict is inversely related to family satisfaction (Aryee et al., 1999) and satisfaction with leisure life (Rice, Frone, & McFarlin, 1992).

Going back to our David example, he is also satisfied with his family situation. He compares his current situation to his previous situation when he had a very long commute to get to the office. Commuting involved waking up much earlier, rushing through grooming, skipping breakfast, and never being able to take the kids to school. He had many arguments with his wife, and the kids gave him a hard time too. His current situation allows him to exert more balance in his life, which in turn reduced conflict with his wife and kids.

3.2.3 Satisfaction with Health and Safety

Work-life balance increases satisfaction in relation to *health and safety*. Employees who benefit from work flexibility are likely to experience decreases in work-related stress. Evidence suggests that stressed employees tend to consume more unhealthy foods and drink more alcohol – both of which are ways to alleviate stress. As such, eating unhealthy foods and heavy alcohol consumption cause health problems (Casey & Grzywacz, 2008; Frone, 1999;

Williams et al., 2006). In contrast, balanced employees are likely to experience greater physical and mental health, thus serving to increase life satisfaction (Greenhaus, Collins, & Shaw, 2003; Haar et al., 2014).

Going back to the David example, working from home helped him reduce the stress caused by the long commute to work and his conflict with his wife and kids. When he had to commute to the office, his blood pressure and cholesterol were high as noted by his family physician. He was overweight because he was eating junk food at work and drinking alcohol during happy hour with his co-workers. His last visit to the family physician several months after he started working from home was all good news. His blood pressure had decreased significantly, he lost a little bit of weight, and his cholesterol was under control.

3.2.4   Satisfaction with Leisure Life

Furthermore, work-life balance contributes to satisfaction in *leisure life*. One can argue that well-balanced employees can easily detach themselves from work and enjoy leisure activities that contribute to personal meaning and development (Lin, Wong, & Ho, 2015). Individuals with work-life balance are likely to experience satisfaction with both their work life and leisure life (Kong, Hassan, & Bandar, 2020).

Let's go back to our David example. Given that he is working from home, he now has much more time to engage in leisure activities with his kids, wife, and friends. Time that he would have spent commuting, he can now use to play games with his children or go on a date with his wife. His friends are envious, saying they wish they had more time to experience leisure *a la* David. David is happier than ever in his leisure pursuits.

3.2.5   Summary

In the preceding section, we explained how work-life balance contributes to domain satisfaction, which in turn feeds into overall life satisfaction. To sum up the domain satisfaction explanation (see Table 3.2), we broke down the evidence by specific life domains, namely marital life, family life, health and safety, and leisure life. That is, we explained how work-life balance contributes to satisfaction in each of those areas. Increasing satisfaction in these life domains contributes to overall life satisfaction.

With respect to *marital life*, the evidence suggests that spending more time working is associated with an increase in work-spouse conflict, which in turn is associated with less marital satisfaction. Hence, reduced work

Table 3.2 *Work-life balance and domain satisfaction*

Dimensions	Subdimensions	Key Findings	References
Marital life satisfaction	Reduced work hours	Spending more time on the job is associated with an increase in work-spouse conflict, which in turn is associated with less marital satisfaction.	Allen et al. (2000); Kossek and Ozeki (1998)
	Flexibility and control over scheduling	Increased control over when and where one works can greatly decrease the conflict between work and marital responsibilities.	Allen et al. (2000); Kossek and Ozeki (1998)
Family life satisfaction	Family satisfaction	Work-life balance increases satisfaction with family life and improves family role performance.	Brough et al. (2014); Frone (2003)
	Less conflict with family members	Work-life balance reduces bidirectional crossover of work-family conflict from one spouse to another.	Westman and Etzion (2005)
	Leisure satisfaction among family members	Work-life balance enhances leisure time and leisure satisfaction among family members.	Johnson, Zabriskie, and Hill (2006)
Health satisfaction	Health satisfaction	Work-life balance has beneficial health effects due to work flexibility.	Casey and Grzywacz (2008)
	Mental health	Individuals with work-life balance participate in salient roles and are mentally healthier because they experience a sense of harmony between physical and mental health.	Haar et al. (2014)
	Low alcohol consumption and problem drinking	Work-life balance reduces work-related stressors that cause elevated alcohol consumption and problem drinking.	Frone (1999)
Leisure life satisfaction	Poor sleep quality	Work-life conflict worsens sleep quality.	Williams et al. (2006)
	Detachment and recovery	Leisure serves to help recover from work stress.	Kong, Hassan, & Bandar (2020); Lin, Wong, and Ho (2015)
	Social interactions	Leisure serves to satisfy social needs.	
	Meaningful activities	Participation in leisure activities bestows personal meaning and enhances personal growth and development.	

hours contribute to satisfaction with marital life. The evidence also suggests that increased control over when and where one works can greatly decrease the conflict between work and marital responsibilities. As such, flexibility and control over scheduling contributes to satisfaction in marital life. In turn, satisfaction with marital life influences life satisfaction overall.

With respect to *family life*, the evidence suggests that work-life balance increases satisfaction with family life and improves role performance in the family domain. Doing so increases family satisfaction, which in turn contributes to life satisfaction. The evidence also suggests a bidirectional crossover of work-family conflict from one spouse to another. That is, problems at work for one employee translates to negative affect that spills over to family life, which in turn spills over onto the spouse amplifying the dissatisfaction with family life. And, of course, this family dissatisfaction becomes a significant contributor to dissatisfaction with life overall. As such, work-life balance serves to minimize conflict between family members, which in turn influences satisfaction with life at large.

Regarding *health and safety*, the evidence also suggests that work-life balance plays a significant role in employee health and safety. Work-life balance has beneficial health effects due to work flexibility. Work flexibility serves to decrease mental stress and physical fatigue, which in turn contributes to satisfaction with one's overall health and fitness. Evidence also suggests that balanced employees are mentally healthier because they experience a sense of harmony between physical and mental health, which in turn contributes to positive mental health. Evidence also suggests that work-life balance reduces work-related stressors that contribute to increased alcohol intake, which in turn increases health and safety. There is also evidence suggesting that work-life conflict takes a toll on sleep quality, which plays an important role in overall health and safety and thus overall life satisfaction.

Finally, regarding *leisure life*, research has shown that participation in leisure activities serves to help employees recover from work stress. Leisure activities also serve to satisfy employees' social needs; and in some cases, leisure participation bestows personal meaning, which in turn contributes to personal development and growth. These factors contribute to satisfaction in leisure life contributing to life satisfaction.

3.3   Work-Life Balance and Stress-Related Outcomes

Poor work-life balance is associated with the following stress-related outcomes, namely emotional exhaustion, psychological distress, and mental health. We will discuss these outcomes in detail in the sections below.

3.3.1   Emotional Exhaustion

Lack of work-life balance causes emotional exhaustion and psychological burnout among employees, which in turn results in poor job performance. There is much evidence demonstrating that work-life conflict results from increased work demand, working hours, shift work, and staff shortages (Brauchli, Bauer, & Hämmig, 2011). Burnout is a condition that occurs when work, combined with additional life pressures, exceeds the ability to cope, resulting in physical and mental distress (Freudenberger, 1974). Burnout is a multi-dimensional syndrome comprising of emotional exhaustion, depersonalization, and a sense of failure to meet organizational goals (Maslach, Schaufeli, & Leiter, 2001). That is, as an individual's emotional exhaustion intensifies, empathy declines, and a low sense of personal accomplishment follows. Burnout has been associated with various forms of job withdrawal – absenteeism, intention to leave the job, and actual turnover. Burnout also is highly predictive of stress-related health outcomes (Maslach, Schaufeli, & Leiter, 2001).

3.3.2   Psychological Distress

Failure to maintain work-life balance causes psychological distress (Allen et al., 2000). There is evidence suggesting that overall distress is associated with work-to-family conflict, which seems to be a major cause of turnover and intentions to quit (Anderson, Coffey, & Byerly, 2002). This means that imbalance may play a major role in overall employee distress, and this distress becomes a major factor in motivating the employee to quit their job. It also increases work-to-family conflict resulting in psychological strain (Brough et al., 2014) and marital and parental distress (Kossek & Ozeki, 1998). More evidence exists suggesting that work-life imbalance causes a great deal of anxiety (Allen et al., 2000; Kossek & Ozeki, 1998). That is, imbalanced employees tend to experience general anxiety much more so than their counterparts.

It is interesting to note that research has discovered that personality can play a moderating effect. Specifically, imbalance tends to generate a higher level of stress for individuals with an external locus of control than for individuals with an internal locus of control (Karkoulian, Srour, & Sinan, 2016). Locus of control is a psychological concept that refers to how strongly people believe they have control over their lives and their surroundings. At work, locus of control typically refers to how employees perceive the causes of their job-related success or failure. This locus-of-control effect may be due to the possibility that individuals with an internal locus of control are likely to better meet role demands in both work and non-work domains, compared to those with an external locus of control.

3.3.3   Mental Health

There is evidence suggesting that a lack of work-life balance decreases mental health. Specifically, employees lacking work-life balance are likely to experience role conflict resulting in decreased job performance and depression (Thomas & Ganter, 1995). Greenhaus et al. (2003) theorized that balanced employees are mentally healthier because they experience a sense of harmony in life and optimal psycho-physiological conditions that enable them to meet the long-term demands of work and nonwork roles.

3.3.4   Summary

In the preceding section on stress-related outcomes, we reviewed evidence suggesting that work-life imbalance is associated with several stress-related outcomes: emotional exhaustion, psychological distress, and mental health (see Table 3.3). Imbalanced employees tend to experience burnout more often than balanced employees. This burnout may be due to work-family conflict, and is indicated by symptoms of emotional exhaustion.

Evidence also suggests that imbalanced employees that experience overall distress due to psychological strain experienced from work-to-family conflict (work interference with family life), often form intentions to quit their job. This psychological distress is also indicated by marital and parental distress and anxiety resulting from work-family conflict. Evidence also suggests that work-life imbalance is associated with depression. Employees become significantly depressed when they fail to meet role demands in their work and nonwork life domains.

3.4   Conclusion

We explained in this chapter how work-life balance contributes to life satisfaction. We pointed out that work-life balance influences life satisfaction directly and indirectly. The direct influence involves satisfaction in multiple domains, positive spillover of domain satisfaction, and minimal role conflict. A high level of life satisfaction is usually a result of satisfaction extracted from multiple life domains. As such, happy employees have to be fully engaged not only in work-life but also in nonwork domains. Satisfaction extracted from multiple life domains increases the

Table 3.3 *Individual work-life balance and stress-related outcomes*

Dimensions	Subdimensions	Key Findings	References
Emotional exhaustion	Psychological burnout	Work-family conflict increases emotional exhaustion, which results in poor job performance.	Brauchli, Bauer, & Hämmig (2011)
Psychological distress	Overall distress	Work-to-family conflict increases turnover intention.	Anderson, Coffey, and Byerly (2002)
		Work-to-life conflict increases psychological strain.	Brough et al. (2014)
	Marital/parental distress	Work-family conflict increases marital/parental distress.	Kossek and Ozeki (1998)
	Anxiety	Work-family conflict increases anxiety.	Allen et al. (2000); Kossek and Ozeki (1998)
Mental health	Depression	Work-family conflict increases depression.	Thomas and Ganter (1995)
	Mental health	Balanced employees are mentally healthier because they experience a sense of harmony in life and optimal psycho-physiological conditions that enable them to meet the long-term demands of work and nonwork roles.	Greenhaus et al., (2003)

chances that both high- and low-order needs are met – high-order needs are growth needs (e.g., the need for self-actualization) and low-order needs are essentially basic needs (the need for food and shelter). Satisfaction extracted from multiple domains increases the likelihood of boosting self-esteem, which in turn plays an important role in life satisfaction. Work-life balance also contributes to life satisfaction through positive spillover of domain satisfaction. That is, life satisfaction increases significantly when positive feelings in one life domain (e.g., social life, family life, leisure life) spills over to work life thus amplifying the summative satisfaction effect on overall life satisfaction. Positive spillover between life domains occurs when the employee applies skills, values, privileges, status, and emotions experienced in one life domain to another. Furthermore, work-life balance contributes to life satisfaction by minimizing stress arising from role conflict, thus reducing overall stress, which in turn helps to maintain an acceptable level of life satisfaction.

We also explained the work-balance effect on life satisfaction by describing to the reader how life satisfaction is increased by increasing satisfaction in specific life domains such as marital life, family life, health and safety, as well as leisure life. As such, activities related to work-life balance (e.g., reduced work hours, flexibility in work schedules and places, engaging in health and fitness programs, and taking time off for vacation) tend to contribute to increased satisfaction in specific life domains (e.g., marital life, family life, health and safety, and leisure life), which in turn spills over into life satisfaction.

We also explained how work-life balance contributes to life satisfaction by reducing stress. We described how balance serves to reduce emotional exhaustion, burnout, work-family conflict, psychological distress, marital and parental distress, anxiety, and depression. As such, work-life balance plays an important role in positive mental health.

What do we make from all of this? This discussion should have impressed upon the reader that work-life balance does indeed play a major role in life satisfaction – balance contributes to life satisfaction and imbalance detracts from it. As such, this discussion sets the stage to explore the interventions that people use to create balance in their lives (i.e., personal interventions). We will discuss these in some detail in the chapters that follow.

References

Allen, T. D., Herst, D. E., Bruck, C. S., & Sutton, M. (2000). Consequences associated with work-to-family conflict: A review and agenda for future research. *Journal of Occupational Health Psychology*, 5(2), 278–308.

Anderson, S. E., Coffey, B. S., & Byerly, R. T. (2002). Formal organizational initiatives and informal workplace practices: Links to work-family conflict and job-related outcomes. *Journal of Management*, 28(6), 787–810.

Aryee, S., Luk, V., Leung, A., & Lo, S. (1999). Role stressors, inter-role conflict, and well-being: The moderating influence of spousal support and coping behaviors among employed parents in Hong Kong. *Journal of Vocational Behavior*, 54(2), 259–278.

Brauchli, R., Bauer, G. F., & Hämmig, O. (2011). Relationship between time-based work-life conflict and burnout. *Swiss Journal of Psychology*, 70(3), 165–174.

Brough, P., Timms, C., O'Driscoll, M. P. et al. (2014). Work-life balance: A longitudinal evaluation of a new measure across Australia and New Zealand workers. *International Journal of Human Resource Management*, 25(19), 2724–2744.

Casey, P. R. & Grzywacz, J. G. (2008). Employee health and well-being: The role of flexibility and work-family balance. *Psychologist-Manager Journal*, 11(1), 31–47.

Edwards, J. R. & Rothbard, N. P. (2000). Mechanisms linking work and family: Clarifying the relationship between work and family constructs. *Academy of Management Review*, 25(1), 178–199.

Freudenberger, H. J. (1974). Staff burn-out. *Journal of Social Issues*, 30(1), 159–165.

Frone, M. R. (1999). Work stress and alcohol use. *Alcohol Research & Health*, 23(4), 284.

Frone, M. R. (2003). Work-family balance. In J. C. Quick & L. E. Tetrick (Eds.), *Handbook of occupational health psychology* (pp. 143–162). Washington, DC: American Psychological Association.

Greenhaus, J. H. & Beutell, N. J. (1985). Sources of conflict between work and family roles. *Academy of Management Review*, 10(1), 76–88.

Greenhaus, J. H., Bedeian, A. G., & Mossholder, K. W. (1987). Work experiences, job performance, and feelings of personal and family well-being. *Journal of Vocational Behavior*, 31(2), 200–215.

Greenhaus, J. H., Collins, K. M., & Shaw, J. D. (2003). The relation between work-family balance and quality of life. *Journal of Vocational Behavior*, 63(3), 510–531.

Greenhaus, J. H. & Powell, G. N. (2006). When work and family are allies: A theory of work-family enrichment. *Academy of Management Review*, 31(1), 72–92.

Haar, J. M., Russo, M., Suñe, A., & Ollier-Malaterre, A. (2014). Outcomes of work-life balance on job satisfaction, life satisfaction and mental health: A study across seven cultures. *Journal of Vocational Behavior*, 85(3), 361–373.

Johnson, H. A., Zabriskie, R. B., & Hill, B. (2006). The contribution of couple leisure involvement, leisure time, and leisure satisfaction to marital satisfaction. *Marriage & Family Review*, 40(1), 69–91.

Karkoulian, S., Srour, J., & Sinan, T. (2016). A gender perspective on work-life balance, perceived stress, and locus of control. *Journal of Business Research*, 69(11), 4918–4923.

Kong, E., Hassan, Z., & Bandar, N. F. A. (2020). The mediating role of leisure satisfaction between work and family domain and work-life balance. *Journal of Cognitive Sciences and Human Development*, 6(1), 44–66.

Kossek, E. & Ozeki, C. (1998). Work-family conflict, policies, and the job–life satisfaction relationship: A review and directions for organizational behavior–human resources research. *Journal of Applied Psychology*, 83(2), 139–149.

Lin, J., Wong, J., & Ho, C. (2015). The role of work-to-leisure conflict in promoting frontline employees' leisure satisfaction. *International Journal of Contemporary Hospitality Management*, 27(7), 1539–1555.

Maslach, C., Schaufeli, W. B., & Leiter, M. P. (2001). Job burnout. *Annual Review of Psychology*, 52(1), 397–422.

Parasuraman, S., Greenhaus, J. H., Rabinowitz, S., Bedeian, A. G., & Mossholder, K. W. (1989). Work and family variables as mediators of the relationship between wives' employment and husbands' well-being. *Academy of Management Journal*, 32(1), 185–201.

Rice, R. W., Frone, M. R., & McFarlin, D. B. (1992). Work–nonwork conflict and the perceived quality of life. *Journal of Organizational Behavior*, 13(2), 155–168.

Sirgy, M. J. & Lee, D.-J. (2016). Work-life balance: A quality-of-life model. *Applied Research in Quality of Life*, 11(4), 1059–1082.

Thomas, L. T. & Ganster, D. C. (1995). Impact of family-supportive work variables on work-family conflict and strain: A control perspective. *Journal of Applied Psychology*, 80(1), 6–15.

Voydanoff, P. (2005). Consequences of boundary-spanning demands and resources for work-to-family conflict and perceived stress. *Journal of Occupational Health Psychology*, 10(4), 491–505.

Westman, M. & Etzion, D. L. (2005). The crossover of work-family conflict from one spouse to the other. *Journal of Applied Social Psychology*, 35(9), 1936–1957.

Williams, A., Franche, R. L., Ibrahim, S., Mustard, C. A., & Layton, F. R. (2006). Examining the relationship between work-family spillover and sleep quality. *Journal of Occupational Health Psychology*, 11(1), 27–37.

PART II

Behavior-Based Personal Interventions of Work-Life Balance

Based on a thorough review of work-life balance (Sirgy & Lee, 2016), we have proposed a set of inter-life domain strategies theorized to increase overall life satisfaction (Lee & Sirgy, 2018). Specifically, work-life balance is conceptualized as a higher-order construct composed of five behavior-based life domain strategies and four cognition-based life domain strategies. The behavior-based strategies are (1) engaging in multiple roles and domains, (2) increasing role enrichment, (3) engaging in behavior-based compensation, (4) managing role conflict, and (5) creating role balance. The cognition-based strategies are: (1) segmenting roles and domains, (2) integrating roles and domains, (3) engaging in value-based compensation, and (4) applying whole-life perspective in decision-making (see Figure PII.1).

The distinction between behavior-based personal interventions of work-life balance and cognition-based interventions is a matter of degree rather than a categorical difference. That is, behavior-based interventions are mostly interventions initiated by some explicit behaviors. The converse applies to cognition-based interventions, they involve a mental process. This is not to say that the mental process does not involve some explicit behaviors. In many cases, cognition-based interventions are manifested in terms of explicit behaviors.

Chapter 4 will discuss how to engage in multiple roles and domains, Chapter 5 on increasing role enrichment, Chapter 6 on engaging in behavior-based compensation, Chapter 7 on managing role conflict, and Chapter 8 on creating role balance.

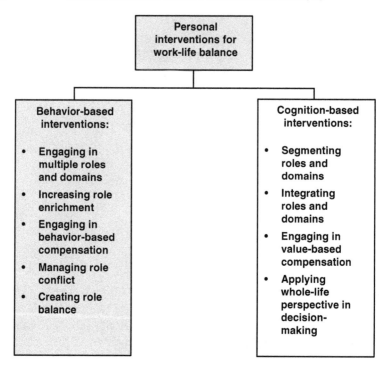

Figure PII.1   Personal interventions for work-life balance

References

Lee, D.-J. & Sirgy, M. J. (2018). What do people do to achieve work-life balance? A formative conceptualization to help develop a metric for large-scale quality-of-life surveys. *Social Indicators Research*, 138(2), 771–791.

Sirgy, M. J. & Lee, D.-J. (2016). Work-life balance: A quality-of-life model. *Applied Research in Quality of Life*, 11(4), 1059–1082.

Sirgy, M. J. & Lee, D.-J. (2018). Work-life balance: An integrative review. *Applied Research in Quality of Life*, 13(1), 229–254.

CHAPTER 4

Engaging in Multiple Roles and Domains

4.1 Engaging in Multiple Roles and Domains

A key behavior-based personal intervention of work-life balance is *role engagement in multiple life domains*. Role engagement in multiple domains refers to an individual's active involvement in social roles of various life domains. Engagement in life domains is likely to produce a positive and fulfilling state of mind characterized by vigor, dedication, and absorption (Schaufeli et al., 2002). Vigor reflects a high level of energy and mental resilience while working. Dedication refers to being strongly involved in one's work by experiencing a sense of significance, enthusiasm, and challenge. Absorption is characterized by complete concentration and engrossment in the task at hand whereby time passes quickly and one has difficulties detaching from the task (Schaufeli & Bakker, 2004).

Role engagement in work and nonwork roles usually produces a positive impact on domain satisfaction, which in turn contributes to overall satisfaction with life (Bakker & Oerlemans, 2011; Bakker et al., 2014). The more the individual is engaged in social roles in a particular life domain, the more likely they will be satisfied with that domain.

Let's consider the example of Tom, a mechanical engineer who is employed at an air conditioning manufacturing plant. He also has a family. A prerequisite to his personal happiness is his full and equal engagement at both work and home. However, Tom is much more absorbed in his mechanical engineering work and not as much at home. At home, he leaves much of the housework and childcare to his wife. However, his wife is not a stay-at-home mom, she has a demanding job too. She is feeling emotionally exhausted because she feels that Tom needs to be more engaged in family life and to help out with household chores and with the kids. Because of his lack of engagement in family life, he and his wife argue a lot; and as such, he does not feel happy at home, which in turn is taking a toll on his satisfaction with life overall.

That is, he is not happy with his life. To increase personal happiness Tom needs to be fully and equally engaged in his work and family roles. Finally, Tom takes corrective action and devotes much more time and energy to meeting role demand in his family life. Doing so made his wife happy, which in turn made him feel equally happy with his family life. This corrective action is, in essence, a work-life balance intervention that served to increase his satisfaction with family life and in turn his life overall.

It is important for individuals to engage in multiple life domains. This is because an individual can only get a limited amount of satisfaction from a single life domain (Ahuvia & Friedman, 1998; Diener, Ng, & Tov, 2008) while overall life satisfaction depends on need satisfaction from multiple life domains (Campbell, Converse, & Rodgers, 1976; Rojas, 2006; Sirgy, 2002). As seen from the Tom example, Tom can only extract a limited amount of satisfaction from his work life. It is not enough to be fully engaged at work and neglect engagement in other important domains such as family life. His intervention – becoming more engaged in family life – was successful in increasing his satisfaction with family life. Feeling satisfied with both work and family roles served to heighten his satisfaction with life overall. Let's see if we can translate this assertion into a set of role engagement principles that can best serve to achieve work-life balance and increased life satisfaction.

4.1.1   Increasing Role Involvement in a Manner Consistent with Life Values

Employees should invest time and energy in social roles consistent with their life values and priorities (Greenhaus & Allen, 2011). That is, individuals should evaluate life goals and invest enough resources to achieve these goals. They can evaluate their values and priorities related to a role in a life domain and adjust allotted time and energy to the role based on these values and priorities (Hirschi, Shockley, & Zacher, 2019). For example, individuals can adjust the allocation of their limited time and energy resources across different social roles based on their life values and priorities. Doing so will help the individual to effectively achieve goals in multiple life domains.

Going back to the Tom example, he finally realized that making his wife happy is an important life goal. As such, his work-life balance intervention was to allot more time and energy to take on household and childcare chores and less time and energy to his job.

4.1.2 Engaging in Multiple Life Domains
to Achieve Positive Balance

Employees should engage in multiple life domains for positive balance. That is, they should engage in multiple life domains that have high personal relevance in order to achieve positive balance. Some people withdraw from life's major roles such as work and family; they care little about all their social roles, approach their roles with little energy, and do not feel intrinsically motivated to engage in role performance. These alienated individuals become disengaged from social life and society at large, and they experience low life satisfaction (Greenhaus, Collins, & Shaw, 2003). One cannot achieve important goals in various life domains by disengagement from those roles embedded in those domains.

The principle of positive balance dictates that life satisfaction can be increased by acceptable role performance in important life domains – *multiple* life domains (Sirgy & Lee, 2016). The idea here is that achieving acceptable levels of satisfaction in multiple domains is key to optimal life satisfaction. Maximizing satisfaction in a salient domain (e.g., work life) contributes little to overall life satisfaction. Achieving moderate-to-high satisfaction in several life domains that are important to the individual (e.g., work life, family life, financial life) works best to boost life satisfaction. The "positive" in "positive balance" reflects "moderate-to-high levels of domain satisfaction," whereas "balance" refers to the idea of achieving comparable "moderate-to-high levels of satisfaction" in several important life domains.

Let's compare Amanda and Susan. Both are college-educated and both work in a digital marketing company. Amanda is a regional sales manager. Susan was recently promoted to vice president of operations – a higher-level position on the managerial ladder. Both are married and have two children of comparable ages. The children even go to the same school and are good friends outside of school, and so are their mothers. Amanda is performing well at work; she is also happy at home. If we were to characterize Amanda's situation in terms of units of satisfaction, she would have "7" units of satisfaction ("1" = very low satisfaction and "10" = very high satisfaction) in her work life and another "7" units of satisfaction in her family life. In other words, she is experiencing "moderate-to-high" satisfaction in both work and family domains. Susan's situation is very different. She loves her new job as a vice president. She is making much more money; she is recognized among her colleagues as "brilliant" and is highly respected. She is now part of upper management. We give her "10" units of satisfaction in her work life (the maximum rating on the satisfaction scale). However, her new position carries with it significantly more responsibilities. Although taking on the additional responsibilities made her feel very satisfied with her job, she feels that she is not adequately meeting family demands. There are many nights when she comes home very late; she often has to skip family vacations; she frequently travels internationally; therefore, she missed important family functions. The kids have been complaining that they hardly see their mom nowadays; her husband is also not very happy with her – he feels somewhat "abandoned" by his wife. Consequently, she feels unhappy in her family life. We rate her level of satisfaction with her family life as "4." Let's now focus on the level of overall life satisfaction that both women are experiencing at the moment. According to the additive model of life satisfaction, we would compute "14" units of satisfaction for both women: Amanda's life satisfaction is "14" satisfaction units: made up of "7" satisfaction units stemming from work life and another "7" units from her family life. Susan is also experiencing "14" units of life satisfaction too: "10" units from her work life and "4" units from her family life. So, based on this life satisfaction algorithm, both women should be equally satisfied with their lives. However, the principle of positive balance contradicts this conclusion, namely that Amanda is likely to be significantly more satisfied with her life than Susan. This is due to the fact that she is experiencing "positive balance," while Susan is lacking in positive balance. Relatively equal amounts of moderately high satisfaction in several important domains contribute to overall life satisfaction, compared to highly variable satisfaction in the same domains (imbalanced domain satisfaction). Low satisfaction in an important life domain can wreak havoc on overall life satisfaction. This is the essence of the principle of positive balance.

In conclusion, the goal for role engagement should be positive balance. That is, employees should be highly engaged in their roles in multiple life domains that are important to achieve moderately high satisfaction in those domains. By the same token, employees should avoid variability in domain satisfaction – imbalance in the satisfaction they experience across domains.

4.1.3 Engaging in Important Roles with Harmonious Passion

Another work-life balance intervention is to engage in important roles with harmonious passion. In this context, the reader should note a distinction between harmonious passion and obsessive passion. First, what is passion? Passion refers to a strong inclination toward an activity or concept that one considers to be an important part of their identity. For example, people with a passion for dancing or swimming do not merely dance or swim. They are "dancers" or "swimmers." When activities become internalized in a person's identity, they reflect either harmonious passion or obsessive passion. A person who engages in a role with harmonious passion tends to identify with that role in an *autonomous* manner. As such, the importance of the role and the activities associated with that role are freely adopted and the activities are pursued for the inherent satisfaction they produce. In contrast, obsessive passion lacks autonomy. In other words, employees who are engaged in their work role with obsessive passion are "workaholics" – they feel compelled to engage in work-related activities because various contingencies are attached to it, such as their own sense of self-worth. As a result, role engagement at work tends to be favored above all other roles and activities in the person's life (Bakker et al., 2014). Workaholics are driven by obsessive passion. In contrast, employees driven by harmonious passion engage in work activities with a high level of vigor, dedication, and a deep sense of absorption; and they do this with a sense of control and in a manner that does not allow work to take over their life. Hence, the recommended work-life balance intervention is to engage in work and nonwork roles with harmonious, not obsessive passion.

Let's illustrate this principle by looking at Anne. Anne is a professor of computer science at an elite university, and she also has children. She is passionate about both her professorial position at the university and her role as a mother. However, a problem has recently arisen. Her role engagement as a mother has turned into an obsession. She feels pressured to be more engaged with her children at their school because of her involvement with the school's Parent-Teachers Association (PTA). That is, she is feeling a great deal of social pressure to conform to the traditional role of being a "good mother." She feels the need to look "good" in the eyes of the other PTA mothers. This social pressure is making her obsessed with her role as mother, to the point that her "mother role" is now controlling every aspect of her life. She is devoting more time, energy, and money to do more for her children at school, ultimately to look good in the eyes of the other PTA mothers. Her teaching, research, and service responsibilities at her university are taking a back seat. Her course evaluations are plummeting; she cannot seem to devote enough time and attention to her research projects, to the point that several of her graduate students have sought other research projects with other mentors. She is not showing up at regularly scheduled committee meetings. In sum, her obsessive passion in her role as a PTA member has caused her to neglect meeting demand in her other roles. Especially her work role. She finally realizes that she is indeed "obsessed" with her PTA role at the expense of her other work duties. This realization has motivated her to act. She reduced her involvement with the PTA and started to rectify her work situation by allotting more time and energy to meet demand in her role as a professor. In essence, her corrective action is to restore work-life balance by realizing that her PTA role has transformed from harmonious to obsessive. Although she reduced her involvement with the PTA she remained involved in her kids' school affairs. In doing so, she transformed her obsessive passion for school activities into harmonious passion.

4.2 Developing a Training Program Guided by the Principle of Role Engagement

Training programs can be developed guided by our understanding of the psychology of role engagement in multiple roles and domains. That is, consultants and experts in work-life balance can introduce the concept of role engagement in their work-life balance training seminars. As such, trainers could instruct employees to increase their involvement in roles that reflect the three principles as captured in Table 4.1: (1) increasing role involvement in a manner consistent with life priorities; (2) engaging in multiple life domains to achieve positive balance; and (3) engaging in an important role with harmonious passion;

With respect to the first principle (*increasing role involvement in a manner consistent with life priorities*), the trainer can help employees apply this principle by guiding employees to invest time, energy, and/or financial resources in social roles consistent with their life values. In other words, employees should be encouraged to evaluate their priorities and adjust time/energy/money investment in roles that have high priority. Workshop participants could be encouraged to list their life goals and rate them on a 10-point scale (Ranging from "1 = Least Important" to "10 = Most Important") (see first two columns in Table 4.2). As shown in Table 4.2, this example subject (let's call him Henry) rated "want my wife to be healthy, happy, and financially secure" as his top priority (Goal Priority score of "10"). His second top priority reflects two life goals" "want my kids to be healthy and financially secure" and "want to be healthy and fit" (Goal Priority scores of "9"). Then participants rate their current expenditure of resources (time/energy/money) on a 10-point scale (ranging from "1 = Very Low Expenditure" to "10 = Very High Expenditure") as seen in column 2 in Table 4.2. As shown in the table, this subject rated his "Current Expenditure of Resources" related to "want my wife to be healthy, happy,

Table 4.1 *Principles of role engagement*

Principles of Role Engagement	Intervention	References
Increase role involvement in a manner consistent with life priorities.	Invest time and psychological energy in social roles consistent with individual life values and priorities. That is, the employee evaluates their priorities and adjusts time and energy investment in roles that have high priority.	Greenhaus and Allen (2011)
Engage in multiple life domains to achieve positive balance.	Engage in multiple life domains high in personal relevance and achieve moderately high satisfaction in those domains. Avoid variability in domain satisfaction	Sirgy and Lee (2016)
Engage in important roles with harmonious passion.	Engage in important roles with greater vigor, dedication, and absorption and do so autonomously.	Bakker et al. (2014)

and financially secure" as "5." Once the table is completed, the individual computes a Surplus/Deficit Score by subtracting the Goal Priority score from Current Expenditure of Resources. Note that this subject had a Deficit Score of "–5" in relation to his top priority goal and "–4" and "–5" scores in relation to his second top priority life goals – "want my kids to be healthy and financially secure" and "want to be healthy and fit."

The Surplus/Deficit Scores reveal what they should do to achieve work-life balance. In this example, Henry should allocate more resources to achieve his top three life goals (which are his marital life, family life, and his health and fitness); and by the same token, he should also allocate fewer resources in his work life. Individuals should allocate more resources to important life domains first, followed by the less important domains. Conversely, individuals should reduce resource allocation in less important and surplus domains, followed by important and surplus domains.

The second principle of role engagement in multiple roles/domains is *positive balance*. Specifically, employees are encouraged to engage in multiple life domains and achieve moderate-to-high amounts of satisfaction in those domains. This translates into two subprinciples namely to engage in multiple life domains high in personal relevance and achieve moderately high satisfaction in those domains; and to avoid variability in domain satisfaction. A training program could be developed around this principle, that employees are likely to experience greater life satisfaction if they are

Table 4.2 *How does Henry make decisions concerning role engagement*

Life Goals	Goal Priority	Current Expenditure of Resources	Surplus/Deficit Score
Want my kids to be healthy and financially secure.	9	5	−4
Want my wife to be healthy, happy, and financially secure.	10	5	−5
Want to be healthy and fit.	9	4	−5
Want my house to be well-maintained and beautiful.	7	3	−4
Want to be successful at my job.	7	10	+3
Want to travel and see the world.	5	2	−3
Want to spend more time with my close friends.	6	3	−3

Notes:
- **Goal Priority**: 10-point rating scale: "1 = Least Important"; "10 = Most Important"
- **Current Expenditure of Resources (Time/Energy/Money)**: 10-point rating scale: "1 = Very Low Expenditure"; "10 = A Great Deal of Expenditure"
- **Surplus/Deficit Score** = (Goal Priority – Current Expenditure of Resources)

fully engaged in multiple life domains that are important to them (e.g., both work and family life). However, we should not expect full engagement in just these two important domains to generate very high satisfaction. In other words, the goal is to achieve moderate-to-high degrees of domain satisfaction across multiple domains, not very high satisfaction. Furthermore, it is important to achieve balance in domain satisfaction. For example, if an employee considers work and family life to be very important (as reflected in their life goals and the priority of these goals in the overall scheme of things), this individual could increase their life satisfaction by achieving moderate-to-high satisfaction in both work life and family life. Both domains should reflect moderate-to-high degrees of satisfaction – equal amounts of "positive" satisfaction in both domains.

The work-life balance instructor could use Table 4.3 to illustrate the principle of positive balance and could encourage participants to complete a blank table reflecting their own perceptions of their domain satisfaction. Note that the example employee who completed this table (let's call him Alfred) has indicated current satisfaction in three life domains or life goals: "want my kids to be healthy and financially secure = +3," "want my wife to be healthy, happy, and financially secure = +3," and "want to be

Table 4.3 *Alfred's attempt to achieve positive balance in domain satisfaction*

Life Goals	Goal Priority	Current Level of Domain Satisfaction
Want my kids to be healthy and financially secure.	9	+3
Want my wife to be healthy, happy, and financially secure.	10	+3
Want to be healthy and fit.	9	+3
Want my house to be well-maintained and beautiful.	7	−2
Want to be successful at my job.	7	+5
Want to travel and see the world.	7	−2
Want to spend more time with my close friends	7	−3

Notes:
- **Goal Priority**: 10-point rating scale: "1 = Least Important"; "10 = Most Important"
- **Current Domain Satisfaction**: 10-point rating scale: "−5 = High Degree of Dissatisfaction"; "+5 = High Degree of Satisfaction"

healthy and fit = +3." According to the positive balance principle, this is good news. He has achieved positive balance in relation to these three life goals (i.e., moderately high amount of satisfaction in these three important goals). However, there is bad news too. He expressed dissatisfaction in relation to three life goals also considered somewhat important: "want my house to be well-maintained and beautiful = −2," "want to travel and see the world = −2," and "want to spend time with my close friends = −3." Based on the principle of positive balance, this situation would be characterized as imbalanced. That is, there is still significant variability in satisfaction in important domains or life goals. As such, Alfred has increased his level of engagement in activities to increase satisfaction in those domains considered important to achieve balance in domain satisfaction. In this situation, the work-life balance instructor would recommend decreasing his level of engagement at work (given the fact that he is pretty happy with his job and can afford to slack off and use some of the time/energy/resources allocated to his job to increase his satisfaction in relation to "maintaining/ beautifying his house," "traveling and seeing the world," and "spending more time with close friends"). Doing so should produce balanced satisfaction in relation to important life goals.

Role engagement in multiple roles/domains also means engaging in important roles with *harmonious passion*. That is, employees have to engage

Table 4.4 *The harmonious/obsessive passion scale applied to work life*

Job-Related Harmonious Passion	Job-Related Obsessive Passion
My job allows me to live a variety of experiences.	I cannot live without my job.
The new things that I discover doing my job allow me to appreciate it even more.	The urge is so strong that I can't help myself from being fully engaged in my job.
My job allows me to live memorable experiences.	I have difficulty imagining my life without my job.
My job reflects the qualities I like about myself.	I am emotionally dependent on my job.
My job is in harmony with the other activities in my life.	I have a tough time controlling my need to be fully engaged in my job.
My job is a passion that I still manage to control.	I have almost an obsessive feeling for my job.
I am completely taken with my job.	My mood depends on me being able to do my job.

Notes:
• *Response Scale*: 7-point rating scale (ranging from "1=Do Not Agree at All" to "7 = Completely Agree")
Source: Adapted from Vallerand et al. (2003), p. 760

in important roles with greater vigor, dedication, and absorption. A training exercise can be developed and administered to employees to educate them about the adverse effects of "workaholism" in that "obsessive engagement in one's job" can wreak havoc on work-life balance and overall life satisfaction.

The core aspect of this training module should involve the administration of the Harmonious/Obsessive Passion Scale as shown in Table 4.4. The measure is adapted from the research of Vallerand et al. (2003). Their research focused on a variety of activities (individual sports such as cycling, jogging, and swimming; team sports such as basketball, hockey, and football; passive leisure such as listening to music and watching movies; active music such as playing the guitar and playing the piano; reading such as reading a novel and reading poetry; active arts such as painting and photography; work/education such as *job engagement* and engagement in academics; and interpersonal relationships such as being with friends or family). We adapted this instrument to focus on job engagement. The goal is to help employee participants gauge their level of harmonious versus obsessive engagement in their jobs. Those whose scores are higher on the job-related obsessive passion items relative to the harmonious passion items are likely to be "workaholics." As such, the administration of this measure could be the basis of a discussion of how obsessive passion in job engagement could play a significant role in poor work-life imbalance.

The reader should note that we recommend the use of the three types of role engagement interventions conjunctively. Here is how it can be done. The workshop participants could evaluate their goal priorities using the Harmonious/Obsessive Passion Scale. Once their life goals are prioritized, resources can be evaluated, and resource surpluses and deficits can be computed in relation to their goal priorities. Finally, the workshop participants can compare their domain satisfaction ratings in relation to the goal priorities to determine how to achieve positive balance through engagement in different roles.

4.3   Conclusion

In this chapter, we made the case that a key behavior-based personal intervention of work-life balance is role engagement in multiple life roles and domains – active involvement in social roles of various life domains. Engagement in different life domains is likely to ensure successful role performance, which in turn contributes to domain satisfaction resulting in overall life satisfaction. Why is it important for individuals to engage in multiple life domains? People can only obtain a limited amount of satisfaction from a single life domain. To feel satisfied with life overall, people have to feel satisfied with their entire spectrum of needs (basic needs such as food and shelter, and growth needs such as social, esteem, and self-actualization needs), and this means engagement in multiple roles and domains.

We also discussed how role engagement in multiple roles/domains is commonly implemented through three types of personal interventions: (1) increasing role involvement in a manner consistent with life values, (2) engaging in multiple domains to achieve positive balance, and (3) engaging in important roles with harmonious passion. What does increasing role involvement in a manner consistent with life values mean? Individuals evaluate life goals and invest enough resources to achieve these goals. They evaluate their values and priorities related to a role in a life domain and adjust allotted time and energy to the role based on these values and priorities.

Engaging in multiple life domains to achieve positive balance means that people engage in multiple life domains that have high personal relevance and strive to achieve balance in domain satisfaction. That is, the principle of positive balance dictates that life satisfaction can be increased by acceptable role performance in important life domains – multiple life domains. Achieving moderate-to-high satisfaction in several life domains that are important to the individual (e.g., work life, family life, financial life) works best to boost life satisfaction. Thus, the "positive" in "positive balance" reflects moderate-to-high levels of domain satisfaction, whereas "balance" refers to the idea of achieving comparable moderate-to-high levels of satisfaction in several important life domains.

The third intervention in role engagement in multiple roles/domains to help achieve work-life balance is engagement in important roles with harmonious passion. We made the distinction between harmonious passion and obsessive passion. When activities become internalized in a person's identity, they reflect either harmonious passion or obsessive passion. A person who engages in a role with harmonious passion tends to identify with that role in an autonomous manner. In contrast, obsessive passion lacks autonomy. "Workaholics" is a good term to characterize obsessive passion in work life.

We also discussed how a training program can be developed reflecting these three principles underlying role engagement. That is, workshops and seminars can be developed and offered to employees to help them achieve work-life balance through role engagement. The instructor should guide participants to increase role involvement in a manner consistent with their life goals and priorities. Table 4.2 captures this role engagement exercise. Participants can also apply the second principle of role engagement – positive balance. Table 4.3 does a good job capturing the gist of this exercise.

Concerning the principle of engaging in important roles with harmonious passion, we recommended that instructors use the Harmonious/Obsessive Passion Scale shown in Table 4.4, which allows participants to measure their degree of passion in their work life. The goal is to identify whether their passion is "harmonious" or "obsessive."

In sum, role engagement in multiple roles and domains is an important step to achieve work-life balance and personal happiness. It is very difficult to achieve balance in life as well as overall life satisfaction without being engaged in multiple roles and domains. Engagement in multiple roles and domains allows an individual to satisfy the full spectrum of needs – both basic and growth needs. To ensure an acceptable level of life satisfaction, people should both engage and succeed in important roles. Successful role performance in multiple roles allows an individual to achieve positive balance in relation to those roles and domains, and positive balance serves to enhance the overall sense of wellbeing. We end by warning about the adverse effects of "obsessive" role engagement. Individuals should not think that successful performance at work alone can bring about happiness. This is an illusion. The reality is that successful performance in *both* work and nonwork roles/domains is key to work-life balance and personal happiness.

References

Ahuvia, A. C. & Friedman, D. C. (1998). Income, consumption, and subjective well-being: Toward a composite macromarketing model. *Journal of Macromarketing*, 18 (2), 153–168.

Bakker, A. B. & Oerlemans, W. (2011). Subjective well-being in organizations. In K. Cameron & G. Spreitzer (Eds.), *The Oxford handbook of positive organizational scholarship*, vol. 49 (pp. 178–189). Oxford: Oxford University Press.

Bakker, A. B., Shimazu, A., Demerouti, E., Shimada, K., & Kawakami, N. (2014). Work engagement versus workaholism: A test of the spillover-crossover model. *Journal of Managerial Psychology*, 29(1), 63–80.

Campbell, A., Converse, P. E., & Rodgers, W. L. (1976). *The quality of American life: Perceptions, evaluations, and satisfactions*. New York: Russell Sage Foundation.

Diener, E., Ng, W., & Tov, W. (2008). Balance in life and declining marginal utility of diverse resources. *Applied Research in Quality of Life*, 3(4), 277–291.

Greenhaus, J. H. & Allen, T. D. (2011). Work-family balance: A review and extension of the literature. In J. C. Quick and L. E. Tetrick (Eds.) *Handbook of occupational health psychology* (pp. 165–183), 2nd edition. Washington, DC: American Psychological Association.

Greenhaus, J. H., Collins, K. M., & Shaw, J. D. (2003). The relation between work-family balance and quality of life. *Journal of Vocational Behavior*, 63(3), 510–531.

Hirschi, A., Shockley, K. M., & Zacher, H. (2019). Achieving work-family balance: An action regulation model. *Academy of Management Review*, 44(1), 150–171.

Rojas, M. (2006). Life satisfaction and satisfaction in domains of life: Is it a simple relationship? *Journal of Happiness Studies*, 7(4), 467–497.

Schaufeli, W. B. & Bakker, A. B. (2004). Job demands, job resources, and their relationship with burnout and engagement: A multi-sample study. *Journal of Organizational Behavior*, 25(3), 293–315.

Schaufeli, W. B., Salanova, M., González-Romá, V., & Bakker, A. B. (2002). The measurement of engagement and burnout: A two sample confirmatory factor analytic approach. *Journal of Happiness Studies*, 3(1), 71–92.

Sirgy, M. J. (2002). *The psychology of quality of life*. Dordrecht: Kluwer Academic Publishers.

Sirgy, M. J. & Lee, D.-J. (2016). Work-life balance: A quality-of-life model. *Applied Research in Quality of Life*, 11(4), 1059–1082.

Vallerand, R. J., Blanchard, C., Mageau, G. A. et al. (2003). Les passions de l'ame: On obsessive and harmonious passion. *Journal of Personality and Social Psychology*, 85(4), 756–767.

CHAPTER 5

Increasing Role Enrichment

5.1 Increasing Role Enrichment

The second behavior-based strategy of work-life balance is role enrichment. *Role enrichment* means that skills and resources in one role can improve or further enhance performance in another role (Greenhaus & Powell, 2006). Individuals experience role enrichment when involvement in one life domain (e.g., work life) helps them understand different viewpoints and develop knowledge, skills, and capabilities in other life domains (e.g., family life). For instance, role enrichment from work to family life helps the employee become a better family member through the transfer of work-related resources to their home (Carlson, Ferguson, & Kacmar, 2016).

Research has documented the effect of role enrichment on overall life satisfaction when roles are integrated (e.g., Olson-Buchanan & Boswell, 2006), when the skills and resource requirements are similar (e.g., Greenhaus & Powell, 2006), and when role performance in one life domain becomes increasingly interdependent with another (e.g., Hanson, Hammer, & Colton, 2006; Ilies, Wilson, & Wagner, 2009; Wayne et al., 2017). Specifically, role enrichment occurs when resources (skills and perspectives, flexibility, and psychological and physical social capital) gained from one role either directly improve performance in the other role or indirectly improve performance by producing positive affect that spills over (Greenhaus & Powell, 2006). For example, successful performance in one role enhances one's self-esteem; this psychological capital contributes to successful performance in another role (e.g., work-family facilitation).

How can one increase role enrichment? Employees can increase role enrichment through the use of their skills, psychological capital, and social capital across all life domains. Let's discuss these in further detail.

5.1.1 The Use of Skills across Life Domains

Employees could apply the *skills* they use at work in nonwork domains such as family life. For example, employees can use negotiation skills they use at work in resolving conflicts among family members. How about transformative leadership skills? This leadership skill can be used in parent-child interactions. How about scheduling and budgeting techniques used at work? These can also be used at home.

Ann is a manager of a fast-food establishment. Through training and experience, she learned many important skills such as selecting and recruiting staff, developing compensation plans, motivating staff to improve job performance, developing a budget and monitoring expenditure, scheduling staff, and supervision techniques. Each of these skills that she learned from her job is put to good use at home. Ann has four children spanning in age from 5 to 16. Through her recruiting responsibilities at work, she learned how to interview potential recruits and look for signs of good character. She uses this skill in making judgments about the friends her kids are socializing with. She wants her kids to befriend other kids who have good character. As such, she encourages her children to spend more time with friends with good character (and less time with friends with not-so-good characters). Her experience with developing compensation plans for her staff was also put to good use at home. She assigns each of her children specific household chores and provides them with a weekly allowance proportional to the amount of time required to complete these chores. Ann uses the same work scheduling template at home. She schedules her children to do the household chores and monitors their performance based on their assigned schedules. Ann also learned how to supervise her staff using a management style that reflects a mix of task orientation and good human relations – ensuring that assigned tasks were completed properly and on time, as well as being emotionally supportive. She applies this leadership skill at home too.

5.1.2 The Use of Psychological Capital across Life Domains

What is *psychological capital*? This concept refers to positive mental traits people build over time enhancing role performance. Examples of these traits include self-esteem, self-confidence, optimism, openness to experience, conscientiousness, social intelligence, and emotional intelligence, among others. Roles can be enriched by transferring these positive mental traits from one role to another and one life domain to another.

Let's go back to Ann, the manager of the fast-food restaurant. She has been very successful as a manager. She has received significant raises over the past several years and several merit awards from upper management. She was also invited several times by upper management to travel to head-quarters to train incoming managers and was compensated extra for doing so. This type of recognition by upper management gave her a large self-esteem boost. She comes across as very confident in her ability to deal with people and any business situation. This boost in self-esteem helped her better manage her family life. When she communicates with her children and husband, she does so with a sense of confidence. Her kids follow through with her requests to do household chores and are very respect-ful. Her children are becoming increasingly well-mannered; she attributes their improved behavior to the boost in her self-confidence. This is a good illustration of role enrichment from work to family life through the boost of psychological capital, namely self-esteem.

5.1.3   The Use of Social Capital across Life Domains

Employees apply their *social capital* across roles and life domains. Social capital refers to interpersonal skills and social networks. In the context of work, an individual with high social capital is a person who effectively manages relationships with other people at work. In the context of family life, social capital may reflect skillful interpersonal interactions with family members, relatives, neighbors, and friends. People with social capital also have better social networks – their circle of social connections is larger with strong social bonds. Research has shown that social capital contributes to role enrichment in significant ways, and that role enrichment plays a sig-nificant part in work-life balance and life satisfaction (ten Brummelhuis & Bakker, 2012).

To illustrate this role enrichment concept, let's revisit the case of Ann, the manager of the fast-food restaurant. One day one of her church mem-bers, Kaitlyn, approached her and confided in her about a family disas-ter – her son was involved in an auto accident that severed his spine and left him paralyzed from the waist down. He would require long-term care and health insurance was not sufficient to cover the cost of long-term care. Ann was moved by Kaitlyn's predicament; she decided to help by launch-ing a fundraising campaign for Kaitlyn's son. In doing so, she tapped into her social capital to conduct a successful campaign. She used her work and social connections to raise $60,000 to cover part of the cost of long-term care. Again, this is an example of role enrichment through the transfer of social capital from one role (being a manager of a local eatery) to another role (being a member of her local church).

5.2 Developing a Training Program Guided by the Principle of Role Enrichment

As discussed in the previous sections, role enrichment is construed as a work-life balance intervention. The intervention involves the use of skills, psychological capital, and social capital to facilitate role performance in another domain (see Table 5.1). Specifically, the skills intervention involves the use of skills commonly applied to facilitate performance at work in nonwork domains and vice versa. For the psychological capital intervention, roles can be enriched by transferring positive mental traits from one role to another and one life domain to another. Similarly, individuals apply their social capital across roles and domains.

Let's see how these role enrichment principles can be used to help employees through a training seminar or workshop. Let's focus first on *skills* that can be transferred from one role to another. We will narrow things down to two life domains for simplicity and effective learning, namely work life and family life; specifically, skills transferred from work life to family life. The training exercise is summarized in Table 5.2.

Ask the participants to list specific skills they learned from their job that they believe may transfer to family life. Ask them to list those skills in Table 5.3. Next, ask them to list specific skills learned at home that would transfer to work life. Use Table 5.4 for this purpose.

Table 5.1 *Role enrichment interventions*

Intervention	Description	References
Skills	Employees could apply the skills they use at work in nonwork domains such as family life, and vice versa	Greenhaus and Powell (2006)
Psychological capital	Roles can be enriched by transferring positive mental traits from one role to another and one life domain to another	Greenhaus and Powell (2006)
Social capital	Employees apply their social capital across roles and life domains	ten Brummelhuis and Bakker (2012)

Table 5.2 *Transfer skills from work to home – identifying application areas*

Skills learned at work	Some illustrative situations that the same skills can be used in the family life	Identify situations that these skills can be applied in your home life
Negotiation skills learned at work	Persuading children	....
	Property transactions	....
	Shopping	....
	Communication during family decisions	....
Leadership skills learned at work	Communication of family values	....
	Coaching children	....
Scheduling skills learned at work	Time management for family life (wake up time, lunch/ dinner time, study/play time, bedtime)	....
	Time management for home duties (shopping, cleaning, maintenance)	....
Budgeting skills learned at work	Allocation of family income	....
	Planning for spending and saving	....
Procurement skills learned at work	Shopping	....
	Stock and inventory management at home	....
Travel logistic skills learned at work	Family travel planning (reservation, logistics, scheduling)	....

Table 5.3 *Specific skills learned from work that can be applied in family life*

Skills learned at work	Can use these skills at home as follows:
Skill 1:	Description of how to use Skill 1 at home: ....
Skill 2:	Description of how to use Skill 2 at home: ....
Skill 3:	Description of how to use Skill 3 at home: ....

Psychological capital can also be transferred from one role to another. Employees can be trained to do so to achieve greater work-life balance and life satisfaction. For simplicity's sake, let's focus on two life domains, namely work life and family life. Table 5.5 can be used to discuss and illustrate the role enrichment principle related to the transfer of psychological

Table 5.4 *Specific skills learned from home that can be applied in work life*

Skills learned at home	Can use these skills at work as follows:
Skill 1:	Description of how to use Skill 1 at work: ....
Skill 2:...................	Description of how to use Skill 2 at work: ....
Skill 3:	Description of how to use Skill 3 at work: ....

Table 5.5 *Ann's transfer of psychological capital from work to home*

Psychological capital gained at work	Transfer of psychological capital to family life
Success at work is attributed to self-esteem and self-confidence in the way the employee performs her job.	Can a boost in self-esteem and self-confidence help her feel happier at home? Discuss.
Success at work is attributed to optimism and positive outlook applied on the job.	Can a boost in optimism and positive outlook help her feel happier dealing with her children and her husband? Discuss.
Caring for coworkers and conscientiousness in carrying out the job.	Can a boost in caring and conscientiousness in carrying out her household chores help bring about a happier family? Discuss.
Openness to new experiences at work.	Can a boost in openness to new experiences at home bring about less conflict and more cohesion among family members? Discuss.
Social and emotional intelligence in work life.	Can a boost in social and emotional intelligence at home bring about less conflict and more cohesion among family members? Discuss.
Conciliation and agreeableness at work.	Can a boost in conciliation and agreeableness at home bring about less conflict and more cohesion in family life? Discuss.

capital from one role to another. The instructor can use the story of Ann, the manager of the fast-food restaurant, to illustrate. We briefly discussed Ann's story in the previous section on psychological capital.

The seminar/workshop instructor can ask the participants to complete Tables 5.6 and 5.7 (below). After completion, encourage a class discussion prompted by the participant's responses.

Like psychological capital, *social capital* can also be transferred from one role to another. Employees can be trained to do so to achieve greater work-life balance and life satisfaction. Go back to Tables 4.2 and 4.3. We illustrated role engagement by first listing a set of life goals that the example individual is pursuing:

Table 5.6 *Specific positive psychological traits facilitating success at work that can be applied in family life*

Positive psychological traits facilitating success at work	The same positive psychological traits applied in family life
Positive Psychological Trait 1: …………………..	Description of how to use Positive Psychological Trait 1 at home to foster family satisfaction: ……………………………………………..
Positive Psychological Trait 2: ………………………..	Description of how to use Positive Psychological Trait 2 at home to foster family satisfaction: ………………………………………………
Positive Psychological Trait 3: ……………………....	Description of how to use Positive Psychological Trait 3 at home to foster family satisfaction: …………………………………………………….

Table 5.7 *Specific positive psychological traits facilitating family cohesion that can be applied in work life*

Positive psychological traits facilitating family cohesion	The same positive psychological traits applied in work life
Positive Psychological Trait 1: …………………..	Description of how to use Positive Psychological Trait 1 at work: ………………………………………
Positive Psychological Trait 2: …………………....	Description of how to use Positive Psychological Trait 2 at work: ……………………………………
Positive Psychological Trait 3: …………………....	Description of how to use Positive Psychological Trait 3 at work: ………………………………………

- Want my kids to be healthy and financially secure (family life);
- Want my wife to be healthy, happy, and financially secure (marital life);
- Want to be healthy and fit (health life);
- Want my house to be well-maintained and beautiful (residential life);
- Want to be successful at my job (work life);
- Want to travel and see the world (leisure life); and
- Want to spend more time with my friends (social life).

The instructor can use the same set of life goals (related to different life domains). The question becomes: How does this person use social capital (more specifically, transfer social capital from one role/domain to another) to make progress in goal attainment? Here is an example the instructor can

Table 5.8 *Transferring social capital from one role/domain to another to achieve life goals*

Important life goals	How can social capital be transferred from one role/domain to another to achieve the stated goal?
Life goal 1:	....
Life goal 2:	....
Life goal 3:	....

use to illustrate how social capital can be transferred from one role/domain to another. Let's focus on the family domain ("want my kids to be healthy and financially secure"). How can this person, let's call him Randy, use social capital that, for example, he was able to harness from the neighborhood (residential life) to help achieve this life goal in his family domain?

Over the years, Randy has established a network of friends in the same neighborhood. He socializes with them and occasionally plays golf with them. One of Randy's children, Sarah, is graduating from college with a degree in computer science. Randy's golf buddies all have upper management positions in companies located within a thirty-mile radius. Sarah would like to live in the same area because she not only has her family there, but she is also dating a local guy with plans to get married and start a family. Randy taps into his social network (his golf buddies) to help Sarah find a suitable IT-related position in a well-established company located nearby. He spreads the word around; and lo and behold, one of his golf buddies mentioned that his company is in the process of recruiting an IT person and asked Randy to send him Sarah's resume. This was followed by a first interview and a second interview that led to a job offer. As such, this example illustrates how social capital was successfully transferred from Randy's residential life to his family life. Doing so enhanced his family wellbeing, which in turn boosted his life satisfaction.

Based on this example, the instructor would then encourage the workshop participants to complete Table 5.8. After completion, the instructor would encourage the class participants to discuss how they can use their own social capital to achieve their life goals.

5.3 Conclusion

This chapter focused on role enrichment as a behavior-based personal intervention. This is a work-life balance intervention. Role enrichment refers to the concept that skills and resources in one role can improve or enhance performance in another role. Employees enrich their roles by transferring their skills, psychological capital, and social capital from one role to the next in work and nonwork domains.

Employees could apply the skills they use at work in nonwork domains such as family life. For example, we discussed how employees use negotiation skills applied at work in resolving conflicts among family members. Psychological capital refers to positive mental traits people build over time that serve to enhance role performance. Examples of these traits include self-esteem, self-confidence, optimism, openness to experience, conscientiousness, social intelligence, and emotional intelligence, among others. Roles can be enriched by transferring these positive mental traits from one role to another and one life domain to another. Employees also apply their social capital across roles and life domains. Social capital refers to interpersonal skills and social networks. In the context of work, an individual with high social capital is a person who effectively manages relationships with other people at work.

We also discussed intervention programs that organizations can institutionalize to achieve higher levels of employee work-life balance through role enrichment. The role enrichment principles can be used to help employees through a training seminar or workshop. Tables 5.2, 5.3, and 5.4 show an example of skill transfer from the work domain to family life and vice versa. Tables 5.5, 5.6, and 5.7 illustrate how psychological capital can be transferred. Finally, Table 5.8 illustrates how social capital can be used in a training course.

In sum, role enrichment is an effective intervention used by people to help them achieve greater work-life balance and personal happiness. Role enrichment is usually accomplished through the transfer of skills, psychological capital, and social capital from one role/domain to another. In other words, people capitalize on certain strengths they have built in the context of one role/domain to address deficits in other roles and life domains. Doing so serves not only to achieve work-life balance but also to increase life satisfaction. Employees can be easily trained to use this personal intervention in the context of a seminar or workshop.

References

Carlson, D. S., Ferguson, M., & Kacmar, K. M. (2016). Boundary management tactics: An examination of the alignment with preferences in the work and family domains. *Journal of Behavioral and Applied Management, 16*(2), 1158–1174.

Greenhaus, J. H. & Powell, G. N. (2006). When work and family are allies: A theory of work-family enrichment. *Academy of Management Review*, 31(1), 72–92.

Hanson, G. C., Hammer, L. B., & Colton, C. L. (2006). Development and validation of a multidimensional scale of perceived work-family positive spillover. *Journal of Occupational Health Psychology*, 11(3), 249–265.

Ilies, R., Wilson, K. S., & Wagner, D. T. (2009). The spillover of daily job satisfaction onto employees' family lives: The facilitating role of work-family integration. *Academy of Management Journal*, 52(1), 87–102.

Olson-Buchanan, J. B. & Boswell, W. R. (2006). Blurring boundaries: Correlates of integration and segmentation between work and nonwork. *Journal of Vocational Behavior*, 68(3), 432–445.

ten Brummelhuis, L. L. & Bakker, A. B. (2012). A resource perspective on the work-home interface: The work-home resources model. *American Psychologist*, 67(7), 545–556.

Wayne, J. H., Butts, M. M., Casper, W. J., & Allen, T. D. (2017). In search of balance: A conceptual and empirical integration of multiple meanings of work-family balance. *Personnel Psychology*, 70(1), 167–210.

CHAPTER 6

Engaging in Behavior-Based Compensation

6.1 Engaging in Behavior-Based Compensation

The third behavior-based inter-domain strategy involving work-life balance is behavior-based compensation. A significant amount of research has been done on the *behavior-based compensation strategy* in industrial/organizational psychology (e.g., Best, Cummins, & Lo, 2000; Staines, 1980). This intervention involves compensating for dissatisfaction in one life domain by increasing engagement in other life domains. That is, satisfaction in one role is interrelated with satisfaction in other roles in a counterbalancing relationship (Greenglass & Burke, 1988).

Specifically, behavior-based compensation means decreased engagement in a dissatisfying role/domain, coupled with increased engagement in alternative roles/domains that produce positive affect (e.g., Clark, 2000; Edwards & Rothbard, 2000; Fereday & Oster, 2010; Freund & Baltes, 2002; Lambert, 1990; Tait, Padgett, & Baldwin, 1989). Individuals choose to participate in alternative roles that they anticipate will produce a certain degree of satisfaction to compensate for the loss of satisfaction in the original domain. By the same token, they disengage from roles in the domain that has produced dissatisfaction.

As such, employees compensate by spending more resources (time, energy, and money) in other domains that they anticipate will produce greater satisfaction. That is, they allocate time, energy, and other resources in an alternative life domain to make up for the satisfaction deficiency in another life domain (Hirschi, Shockley, & Zacher, 2019).

Florence is a business executive in a telecommunication company. She is also having marital problems. She and her husband are discussing divorce. As such, her marital satisfaction has drastically decreased. Her satisfaction with her life overall has also plummeted because of the increased dissatisfaction in her marital life. She now spends much more time at work. She recently accepted an international travel assignment that would allow her to immerse herself in work and be away from the headaches associated with her marital life. The travel assignment is also making her feel important at work, and she is being recognized by upper management for her stellar job performance and commitment to the company. Such recognition is increasing her satisfaction in her work life, which in turn is compensating for the dissatisfaction she is experiencing in her marital life. In doing so, she manages to maintain her overall life satisfaction at an acceptable level.[1]

How can employees practice behavior-based compensation? They can effectively compensate by reallocating resources (time, energy, and money) across domains. That is, resources are decreased in domains in which the individual is currently dissatisfied and reallocated to domains in which they anticipate future satisfaction.

6.1.1 Reallocate Time to Compensate

A behavior-based compensation intervention involves reallocating *time* to a role in which the person has found satisfying in the past and anticipates more future satisfaction through increased role engagement. That is, the person allocates more time to the satisfying role and less time to the dissatisfying role.

Consider Bill's situation. Bill is a software engineer. He works for a social networking company. However, recently his work demand has been increasing exponentially and the company's work culture has turned toxic. His boss is an ass with a very strict management philosophy: he becomes very critical of staff members who don't complete their assigned projects "perfectly" and "on time." He also has zero tolerance for errors and delays and does not hesitate to publicly humiliate Bill and any of his colleagues if and when they falter. Bill has been going to church lately. He has found a certain serenity and contentment in church. The fellowship at the church is very positive, and he recently joined the church choir. Singing in the choir has been very uplifting for Bill. As such, he decided to spend

---

[1] Please note that previously we discussed the principle of multiple role engagement which states that individuals with a balanced life tend to be fully engaged in multiple roles. Engaging in a single role does not significantly contribute to overall life satisfaction. When people become engaged in only one life domain (e.g., work life), they are not likely to experience overall life satisfaction because the amount of satisfaction that we can extract from a single life domain is limited. It may seem like we are directly contradicting the principle of satisfaction in multiple domains" by making a case for the "principle of behavior-based compensation" as discussed here. The reader has to keep in mind that, although some of these principles may conflict, they do operate under various conditions. The trick is to become aware of those optimal conditions related to each principle.

more time at church, not only participating in the choir but also with the youth ministry. Additionally, he met with his supervisor and requested to be a participant in a job-sharing program that the company recently announced. This program allows two software engineers to staff one position. His boss agreed but reluctantly. He can afford the reduction in pay given the fact that he does not have a family and he's been living within his means. Hence, the job-sharing program should him allow to *reduce his time at work* and reallocate this time to church activities. As a result, *allocating more time* for church activities is serving him well by compensating for the dissatisfaction he has been experiencing at work lately. This dissatisfaction is now compensated by increasing his satisfaction in church life. Such compensation serves to maintain an acceptable level of overall life satisfaction.

6.1.2   Reallocate Energy to Compensate

The focus here is on reallocating *energy*, not time. That is, when people become dissatisfied with a specific role in a specific life domain, they compensate for the loss of satisfaction by increasing effort expended in another role or domain.

Going back to Bill, the software engineer, instead of reallocating time, he decides to reallocate some of the energy he previously devoted to work. He does so by "working smart" instead of "working hard." He does this by teaming up with other colleagues who work collaboratively to check one another's programming output. This collaborative effort works best to ensure quality control while reducing the amount of time each engineer takes to test and retest the programming output. Thus, "working smart" has allowed him to lighten his workload; now, he is putting less effort and energy into his job. He can now put more energy into his church participation. Increased effort in church participation does not necessarily mean increased hours. It means increased effort and involvement. Instead of spending more time on choir activities and youth ministry, he puts more effort in. He does this by not simply attending church services but by also participating in every aspect of the service – praying, chanting, baptism, communion, bible study, and fellowship. Consequently, allocating more energy for church activities is serving him well by compensating for the dissatisfaction he has been experiencing at work lately. Again, this dissatisfaction is now compensated for by increasing his satisfaction in church life, and such compensation allows him to maintain his satisfaction with life overall.

6.1.3 Reallocate Financial Resources to Compensate

In the previous two subsections, we described how people attempt to balance their lives by reallocating time and energy – spending more time and energy in roles producing satisfaction and less in roles causing dissatisfaction. A similar case can be made concerning financial resources. That is, people attempt to compensate for the dissatisfaction they experience in certain roles and domains by *spending more money* in roles and domains producing high levels of satisfaction. Role engagement comes in the form of spending time, energy, and in many cases money.

Going back to Bill's case. Remember how Bill compensated for his dissatisfaction at work by reducing his time at work and increasing his time and effort devoted to church activities? Bill can engage in church activities not only in terms of increased time and effort but also by money spent on church activities. He decides to increase his church contribution by an affordable amount and spend less money eating and drinking out with his coworkers. As such, the money budgeted for food and drinks for lunch and happy hour after work is now going to the church. Doing so makes him more satisfied with church life to compensate for the dissatisfaction he is feeling at work. This money compensation intervention is helping him sustain an acceptable level of wellbeing.

6.2 Developing a Training Program Guided by the Principle of Behavior-Based Compensation

In the preceding section we discussed a work-life balance strategy that many commonly use in the form of behavior-based compensation. That is, people compensate for dissatisfaction they experience in certain roles by spending more time, energy, and/or financial resources in roles that produce high levels of satisfaction (see Table 6.1). Doing so allows the individual to maintain an acceptable level of overall life satisfaction.

We also made the case that compensation through reallocation of time, energy, and money are three different interventions. That is, they are not used simultaneously, they are used independently. However, there may be overlap among these three compensation strategies in some cases.

Now let us explore how these three principles can be developed into a training program to help employees achieve work-life balance. The work-life balance training program can include a module on how to reallocate time. The instructor could show Table 6.2 as a slide and explain what is being illustrated. The example shown in Table 6.2 focuses on Carmen,

Table 6.1 *Behavior-based compensation interventions*

Intervention	Description	References
Reallocate time.	Spend more time in roles producing satisfaction and less time in roles causing dissatisfaction.	Freund and Baltes (2002); Hirschi, Shockley, and Zacher (2019)
Reallocate energy.	Spend more energy in roles producing satisfaction and less energy in roles causing dissatisfaction.	Freund and Baltes (2002)
Reallocate financial resources.	Spend more financial resources in roles producing satisfaction and less in roles causing dissatisfaction.	Freund and Baltes (2002)

who is a college professor. The scores in the table demonstrate her emotional experiences in various life domains (family, marital, health/safety, residential, work, leisure, and social). She regards her marital life as most important (a score of "10" on a 10-point importance rating scale), followed by both her family life (a score of "9") and her health and safety (a score of "9"). The other domains (residential, work, leisure, and social) are less important (scores ranging from "5" to "7").

Although marital and family life are on top of her priority list, she reports that she is very unhappy in her marital life (a score of "-5" on a 10-point scale varying from -5 to +5) and moderately unhappy in her family life ("-3"). Column C is the product of Domain Importance and Domain Satisfaction. Multiplying the scores in the first two columns allows us to see what levels of satisfaction or dissatisfaction Carmen is experiencing across all domains. In this case, we see that Carmen is clearly dissatisfied in her marital life ("-50") followed by family life ("-27"). Dissatisfaction in these life domains is causing her to feel a great deal of dissatisfaction with life overall. She decides to divorce her husband and spend less time with family. She decides that her teenage children should spend more time with their father; they don't need her that much given the conflict in family life. Currently, she is spending 25 percent of her weekly time with family, and 15 percent with her husband. She decides to deal with her dissatisfaction in her family life by spending only 5 percent with family and 0 percent with her husband (given the pending divorce). To ensure that she maintains an acceptable level of overall life satisfaction she decides to spend more

Table 6.2 *Carmen's reallocation of time to achieve work-life balance*

Life Domain	Domain Importance (A)	Domain Satisfaction (B)	C = A x B	Current Expenditure of Time	Ideal Expenditure of Time
Family life	9	-3	-27	25%	5%
Marital life	10	-5	-50	15%	0%
Health and safety	7	-1	-7	5%	5%
Residential life	7	+3	+21	3%	15%
Work life	7	+2	+14	45%	55%
Leisure life	5	+1	+5	2%	10%
Social life	6	+1	+6	5%	10%
TOTAL				100%	100%

Notes:

- **Domain Importance**: 10-point rating scale: "1 = Least Important"; "10 = Most Important"
- **Current Domain Satisfaction**: 10-point rating scale: "-5 = High Degree of Dissatisfaction"; "+5 = High Degree of Satisfaction"
- **Current Expenditure of Time (Weekly)** = percent of current time allocated to activities within the specified domain
- **Ideal Expenditure of Time (Weekly)** = percent of ideal time that should be allocated to activities within the specified domain

Table 6.3 *Reallocating time to achieve work-life balance*

Life Domain	Domain Importance (A)	Domain Satisfaction (B)	C = A x B	Current Expenditure of Time	Ideal Expenditure of Time
Life domain 1:	...	...	...	...	...
Life domain 2:	...	...	...	...	...
Life domain 3:	...	...	...	...	...
Life domain 4:	...	...	...	...	...
Life domain 5:	...	...	...	...	....
Life domain 6:	...	...	...	...	...
Life domain 7:	...	...	...	...	...
TOTAL	...	...	...	...	...

Notes:
- **Domain Importance**: 10-point rating scale: "1 = Least Important"; "10 = Most Important"
- **Current Domain Satisfaction**: 10-point rating scale: "-5 = High Degree of Dissatisfaction"; "+5 = High Degree of Satisfaction"
- **Current Expenditure of Time (Weekly)**: percent of current time allocated to activities within the specified domain
- **Ideal Expenditure of Time (Weekly)** = percent of ideal time that should be allocated to activities within the specified domain

time in those domains she is feeling somewhat satisfied in; and in doing so she regains some degree of satisfaction in those positive domains. These domains are residential, work, leisure, and social. That is, she decides to increase her weekly time allotment in these life domains by 12 percent in residential life (from 3 percent to 15 percent), 10 percent in work life (from 45 percent to 55 percent), 8 percent in leisure life (from 2 percent to 10 percent), and 5 percent in social life (from 5 percent to 10 percent).

After going through this scenario, the instructor can ask each participant to complete Table 6.3 on their own, after which the instructor would prompt a discussion based on the participants' responses.

The instructor can also encourage participants to engage in a similar exercise to discuss and explain how they can achieve work-life balance by reallocating effort and financial resources using Tables 6.4 and 6.5.

Table 6.4 *Reallocating effort to achieve work-life balance*

Life Domain	Domain Importance (A)	Domain Satisfaction (B)	C = A x B	Current Expenditure of Effort	Ideal Expenditure of Effort
Life domain 1:	...	...	...	...	...
....					
Life domain 2:	...	...	...	...	...
....					
Life domain 3:	...	...	...	...	...
....					
Life domain 4:	...	...	...	...	...
....					
Life domain 5:	...	...	...	...	...
....					
Life domain 6:	...	...	...	...	...
....					
Life domain 7:	...	...	...	...	...
....					
TOTAL	...	...	...	...	...

Notes:
- **Domain Importance**: 10-point rating scale: "1 = Least Important"; "10 = Most Important"
- **Current Domain Satisfaction**: 10-point rating scale: "–5 = High Degree of Dissatisfaction"; "+5 = High Degree of Satisfaction"
- **Current Expenditure of Effort (Weekly)**: percent of current amount of effort allotted to activities within the specified domain
- **Ideal Expenditure of Effort (Weekly)** = percent of ideal amount of effort that should be allotted to activities within the specified domain

6.3   Conclusion

In this chapter we discussed how people try to achieve work-life balance and maintain an acceptable level of life satisfaction by allotting more time, energy, and financial resources in roles and life domains that can produce a high level of satisfaction. By the same token, they attempt to decrease their involvement in roles and domains that are dissatisfying.

We also discussed intervention programs that organizations can institutionalize to help their employee achieve greater work-life balance through behavior-based compensation. We used Tables 6.2 and 6.3 to illustrate how employees can be trained to reallocate their time to achieve work-life balance. This can be done by having the workshop participants rate the relative importance of their life domains and indicate their level of

Table 6.5 *Reallocating financial resources to achieve work-life balance*

Life Domain	Domain Importance (A)	Domain Satisfaction (B)	C = A x B	Current Money Expenditure	Ideal Money Expenditure
Life domain 1:	...	...	...	...	...
....					
Life domain 2:	...	...	...	...	...
....					
Life domain 3:	...	...	...	...	...
....					
Life domain 4:	...	...	...	...	...
....					
Life domain 5:	...	...	...	...	...
....					
Life domain 6:	...	...	...	...	...
....					
Life domain 7:	...	...	...	...	...
....					
TOTAL	...	...	...	...	...

Notes:

- **Domain Importance:** 10-point rating scale: "1 = Least Important"; "10 = Most Important"
- **Current Domain Satisfaction:** 10-point rating scale: "−5 = High Degree of Dissatisfaction"; "+5 = High Degree of Satisfaction"
- **Current Expenditure of Money (Weekly):** percent of current amount of money spent on activities within the specified domain
- **Ideal Expenditure of Money (Weekly)** = percent of ideal amount of money that should be allotted to activities within the specified domain

satisfaction in each domain after which they list their current expenditure of time in each domain followed by their ideal allotment of time. After identifying satisfying and dissatisfying domains, participants are then encouraged to compensate by making adjustments in their time allotment in the various domains – allot more time to satisfying domains and less time to dissatisfying domains.

We also discussed how instructors can encourage participants to engage in a similar exercise to explain how they can achieve work-life balance by reallocating effort and financial resources using Tables 6.4 and 6.5.

In sum, employees can learn to increase their work-life balance by spending more time, energy, and other resources in domains that have produced satisfaction in the past; and less time/energy/money in domains that produced dissatisfaction. Doing so allows them to maintain an acceptable level of life satisfaction by compensating for the satisfaction deficit in certain domains and their adverse effects on overall life satisfaction.

References

Best, C. J., Cummins, R. A., & Lo, S. K. (2000). The quality of rural and metropolitan life. *Australian Journal of Psychology*, 52(2), 69–74.

Clark, S. C. (2000). Work/family border theory: A new theory of work/family balance. *Human Relations*, 53(6), 747–770.

Edwards, J. R. & Rothbard, N. P. (2000). Mechanisms linking work and family: Clarifying the relationship between work and family constructs. *Academy of Management Review*, 25(1), 178–199.

Fereday, J. & Oster, C. (2010). Managing a work-life balance: the experiences of midwives working in a group practice setting. *Midwifery*, 26(3), 311–318.

Freund, A. M. & Baltes, P. B. (2002). Life-management strategies of selection, optimization and compensation: measurement by self-report and construct validity. *Journal of Personality and Social Psychology*, 82(4), 642–662.

Greenglass, E. R. & Burke, R. J. (1988). Work and family precursors of burnout in teachers: Sex differences. *Sex Roles*, 18(3), 215–229.

Hirschi, A., Shockley, K. M., & Zacher, H. (2019). Achieving work-family balance: An action regulation model. *Academy of Management Review*, 44(1), 150–171.

Lambert, S. J. (1990). Processes linking work and family: A critical review and research agenda. *Human Relations*, 43(3), 239–257.

Staines, G. L. (1980). Spillover versus compensation: A review of the literature on the relationship between work and nonwork. *Human Relations*, 33(2), 111–129.

Tait, M., Padgett, M. Y., & Baldwin, T. T. (1989). Job and life satisfaction: A reevaluation of the strength of the relationship and gender effects as a function of the date of the study. *Journal of Applied Psychology*, 74(3), 502.

CHAPTER 7

Managing Role Conflict

7.1 Managing Role Conflict

Individuals that successfully manage role conflict are likely to experience work-life balance. When they manage role demand in multiple domains, they are less likely to experience psychological stress and role overload. Doing so helps guard against decreases in overall life satisfaction.

Much research has documented the fact that work-life balance is achieved when there is little-to-no role conflict between social roles (e.g., Greenhaus & Beutell, 1985; Rau & Hyland, 2002). Role conflict reflects the degree to which role responsibilities in one life domain and another life domain are incompatible (Greenhaus & Beutell, 1985). As such, the demands of one role make the performance of the other role more difficult (Netemeyer, Boles, & McMurrian, 1996). Individuals experience role conflict when it becomes increasingly difficult to perform each role successfully due to conflicting demands on time and energy (Greenhaus & Beutell, 1985). Employees experience work-to-family conflict (i.e., work interfering with family life) when their work schedule often conflicts with their family life and/or when their work takes up family time. Alternatively, they experience family-to-work conflict (i.e., family interfering with work life) when their family events are scheduled at times that often conflict with their work schedule and/or when their personal life takes up time already allotted for work (Grandey & Cropanzano, 1999). Research has shown that work-family role conflict is associated with life dissatisfaction (e.g., Edwards & Rothbard, 2000; Sturges & Guest, 2004); low martial and family satisfaction; and symptoms of ill-being, both mental and physical (e.g., Parasuraman, Greenhaus, & Granrose, 1992).

People often experience role conflict between work and family roles because the demands of work and family roles are inherently incompatible. This principle is supported by substantial research guided by the conservation of resources model (e.g., Fisher, Bulger, & Smith, 2009;

Grandey & Cropanzano, 1999; Hobfoll, 1989). The model suggests that individuals are motivated to seek and conserve resources to meet role demand in their various domains. As such, work-life balance is difficult to achieve given role conflict. Role conflict arises when the resources needed to meet the demands of one role are used at the expense of another. The model also suggests that work-life balance can be enhanced when resources obtained from one domain can be used to facilitate role performance in another domain. Frone (2003) made a distinction between two forms of work-family conflict. The direction of the adverse effect stemming from one domain over the other has to be identified. As such, the factors related to the interference of work life on family life are not the same as factors related to the interference of family life on work life (see also Carlson, Kacmar, & Williams, 2000; Friedman & Greenhaus, 2000; Greenhaus & Beutell, 1985).

How can employees manage role conflict? Employees can implement the following interventions: (1) matching role demand with role resources, (2) managing time, and (3) managing stress.

7.1.1 Matching Role Demand with Role Resources

Employees experience role conflict because they cannot devote enough time or energy to perform their roles successfully. To reduce role conflict, people have to match role demand and resources across life domains (Allen, 2001). For example, if there is too much work interference on family life, then the individual should reduce their workload by using a set of family-friendly programs at work (e.g., flexible schedule, flexible workplace, alternative job arrangement, etc.). Alternatively, they can find other means and resources that can be used to meet role demand (e.g., obtaining help from others, using automated home appliances). They can also prioritize and use their time and energy more efficiently in their various work and nonwork roles.

Consider the case of Tiffany. Tiffany is a single mother with a 3-year-old daughter. She works at a large supermarket in her local area as a cashier. She feels fortunate that she has the day shift (9:00 a.m. to 5:00 p.m.) to ensure that she has time for her daughter in the evening. However, there is a significant problem, namely the cost of childcare. She cannot afford childcare on the wages she makes at the supermarket. That is, she lacks the financial resources to meet her role demand as a mother and caretaker. How did she manage? She had to improvise. She sought assistance from her mother, her neighbors, her friends, and her former husband. She had to beg and plead to have people in her social network take care of her daughter. And this scramble to find someone to babysit caused significant stress in her life. This role conflict is a direct result of a mismatch between role demand and resources. Tiffany was able to achieve work-life balance when the grocery chain initiated a childcare program. The company is now offering to cover the cost of childcare services, which was a blessing to Tiffany. Now she can meet her role demand as a mother and caretaker, since resources and role demand match. As such, she is making progress toward work-life balance.

7.1.2 Managing Time

Role conflict frequently occurs when time demands associated with participation in one role interfere with participation in another role (Greenhaus & Beutell, 1985). That is, work-family conflict arises from problems scheduling time devoted to work and family roles, or both (Frone, Russell, & Cooper, 1992). Much research has shown that good time management can reduce work-family conflict (Adams & Jex, 1999).

Effective time management often involves using a paper or digital planner to make to-do lists and check off each task as it is completed (Macan et al., 1990). Of course, an important ingredient in scheduling is being cognizant of scheduling conflicts. That is, one should avoid scheduling projects and events that may conflict with one another (Epstein & Kalleberg, 2004).

Dave, a manager of a clothing boutique, has been experiencing a great deal of work-family conflict. He is experiencing a high level of stress because he can't seem to meet both his work and family obligations. He gave his predicament a lot of thought. He realized that a significant part of the problem is a lack of time management – he commits to doing things at home and work at times that conflict with one another. What to do? He decided to download a calendar app on his phone and record every commitment he makes (work and nonwork). The trick is being vigilant in checking his calendar before making any work or nonwork commitments. Previously, he would often accept invitations without writing them down. He relied on his memory, which of course is fallible, especially when he is stressed and distracted. Now the digital calendar is on his mobile phone and is easily accessible in most situations. He now tries to check his calendar before scheduling anything new, record all invitations as soon as he accepts them, and check it frequently throughout the day to avoid missing events. He is also using the alarm on his phone to alert him of an impending scheduled event. Using the phone calendar has been instrumental in reducing role conflict due to a lack of time management.

7.1.3   Managing Stress

There are many stress management techniques discussed in the stress management research literature. Examples of popular interventions include regular exercise, meditation and praying, and social support.

Research has shown that leaders who *exercise regularly* have increased stamina and mental focus compared to those who do not exercise or who exercise less frequently (Leiter & Maslach, 2005; Neck & Cooper, 2000). Some research has shown that unwillingness to exercise may be a result of role conflict – conflict between work and family roles does not leave the individual with enough time or energy to exercise (e.g., Allen & Armstrong, 2006; Grace et al., 2006; Grzywacz & Marks, 2001; Roos et al., 2007). Conversely, research has also shown that those who exercise frequently report less work-family conflict. For example, a study (Clayton et al., 2015) was able to demonstrate that physical exercise (i.e., physical activity that is planned, structured, repetitive, and purposeful) has indirect effects on work-family conflict by increasing self-efficacy in managing work-family conflict and decreasing psychological strain. That is, the study findings suggest that physical exercise heightens one's belief that they can manage their work and family lives (i.e., self-efficacy), and as such, they can better cognitively manage work-family conflict. Wellness programs have become fashionable in the corporate world, and physical fitness is now an entrenched and well-established work-life balance program (Kossek, Ozeki, & Kosier, 2001). Consider the following companies as an example. Both Zappos.com and Google were named in *Fortune*'s "100 Best Companies to Work For." Among other perks, both companies provide employees with on-site fitness programs (e.g., yoga classes). Considerable evidence has shown that wellness programs do make a positive impact on reducing absenteeism and health insurance premiums as well as increasing job satisfaction, employee morale, and employee retention (DeGroot & Kiker, 2003; Parks & Steelman, 2008).

How about *meditation*? Consider the following study by Kiburz, Allen, and French (2017). The study examined the effectiveness of a brief mindfulness-based training intervention that involved a one-hour workshop followed by thirteen days of behavioral self-monitoring. The goal of the study was to reduce work-family conflict, and the intervention was successful in doing so. Specifically, those who participated in the intervention experienced greater mindfulness, less work-to-family conflict, and less family-to-work conflict than did those who did not participate in the intervention. *Praying* can be considered a form of meditation. A study conducted on female, Muslim academicians in Malaysia (Achour, Grine, & Mohd Nor, 2014) found that a significant number of participants reported that turning to religion in times of need helped manage their stress. The participants asserted that they turn to "Allah" to help solve all problems related to family, work, and others. From this, it is clear that praying can be an effective strategy to deal with high demand from multiple roles.

Social support can also reduce work-family conflict and minimize the detrimental effects of role conflict on health and wellbeing. Social support has been proven to have a beneficial impact on reducing psychological strain, increasing job and family satisfaction, and reducing work-family conflict (e.g. Byron, 2005; Drummond et al., 2017; O'Driscoll & Brough, 2010). The converse is also true – lack of social support can exacerbate work-family conflict (Ayman & Antani, 2008), which in turn increases psychological strain and reduces satisfaction in both work and family life. Social support is usually provided by a spouse or a close family member. Research has shown that a supportive partner is usually an important resource to reduce strain experienced in the family domain and alleviate family-to-work conflict (e.g., Frone, Yardley, & Markel, 1997; Greenhaus & Beutell, 1985; Voydanoff, 2005). Given that family distress is associated with family-to-work conflict, a supportive partner acts as a buffer to reduce family distress. Consider the Malaysian study on women academics (Achour, Grine, & Mohd Nor, 2014). In addition to using religion as a coping strategy to deal with work-family conflict, the women also identified social support as a key strategy to deal with the demands involved with multiple roles.

7.2   Developing a Training Program Guided by the Principle of Managing Role Conflict

Role conflict occurs when an employee fails to meet demand in nonwork life domains because of role engagement in work life, and vice versa. Managing role conflict helps employees achieve work-life balance. When they manage role demand in multiple domains, they are less likely to experience psychological stress and role overload. Doing so helps guard against decreases in overall life satisfaction.

How can employees manage role conflict? Common interventions deemed successful include matching role demand with role resources, managing time, and managing stress (see Table 7.1).

Table 7.1 *Managing role conflict to achieve work-life balance*

Intervention	Description	References
Matching role demand with role resources.	Reduce role demand in roles that lack adequate resources or increase role resources to meet role demand.	Allen (2001) Green and Skinner (2005)
Managing time.	Use time management techniques such as downloading a calendar app on a mobile phone, marking all committed events on the calendar, checking the calendar before making future commitments, and using the phone alarm to provide alerts about impending events.	Frone, Russell, and Cooper (1992)
Managing stress.	There are many stress management techniques that include regular exercise, meditation and praying, and social support.	Drummond et al. (2017); Kiburz, Allen and French (2017); Roos et al. (2007)

Matching role demand with role resources involves the reduction of role demand in roles that lack adequate resources or increasing role resources to meet role demand. Managing time involves the use of time management techniques and tools such as downloading a calendar app on a mobile phone, marking all committed events on the calendar, checking the calendar before making future commitments, and using the phone alarm to provide alerts about impending events. Managing stress involves the use of stress management techniques such as regular exercise, meditation and praying, and social support.

Allow us to be more specific. Let's focus more on the first intervention, namely *matching role demand with role resources*. This involves the reduction of role demand in roles that lack adequate resources or increasing role resources to meet role demand. Let's focus on a specific life domain, let's say family life. Consider Melissa, she is the director of a regional office employing fifteen pharmaceutical sales representatives. The regional office belongs to a large pharmaceutical company. She is also the mother of five children spanning in age from 5 to 16, all girls. She is married to a cardiologist named Phil. As such, her husband is constantly on call and is extremely busy attending to his patient's medical needs. In addition to her work role as the director of regional pharmaceutical sales, Melissa assumes several other roles in the family domain: mother, wife, chauffeur, cook, shopper, household accountant, member of the school's Parent-Teacher Association (PTA), president of the neighborhood homeowners' association (HOA), and social events coordinator. Now examine Table 7.2.

Note that Melissa perceives that she has the required resources to perform her roles as a mother, wife, accountant, PTA member, president of the HOA, and social events coordinator. Her scores are "0" in the Surplus versus Deficit column of the table. In contrast, there is a deficit of resources in relation to her roles as a chauffeur, cook, and shopper. Her role as a shopper has the greatest deficit. As such, if Melissa obtains the additional resources she needs in those roles with a deficit, she is very likely to manage her role conflict and reduce stress. Reducing stress should help her achieve greater work-life balance and overall life satisfaction. However, ascertaining the levels of surplus/deficit should not be viewed as the ultimate guide to decision-making. The final decision regarding allocating resources should also consider role priority. That is, some roles are perceived to be more important than others. When we take into account Melissa's perception of the degree of importance of these roles (i.e., role priority), we conclude that the allocation of resources to these roles could be prioritized: the "shopper role" should take greater priority, followed by the "chauffeur role" and the "cook role," respectively.

The instructor can use a similar template to encourage the workshop participants to engage in a similar exercise. This template is shown in Table 7.3.

Now let us turn to *time management* and discuss its ramifications in terms of work-life balance. There are many time management techniques. These include downloading a calendar app on a mobile phone, marking all committed events on the calendar, checking the calendar before making future commitments, and using the phone alarm to provide alerts about impending events. Consider the case of Daniella. She seems to be continuously running into time management problems. She often finds herself missing meetings due to a combination of factors including that she schedules meetings that conflict with one another; she forgets to record a scheduled meeting in her calendar; and on occasion, she forgets to look at her calendar to check her already scheduled meetings. Part of her time management problem is that she uses three separate notebook calendars, one at her office on her desk, another in her purse, and another at home. She often forgets to synchronize the three calendars resulting in poor time mismanagement.

Table 7.2 *Melissa's attempt to manage role conflict by matching role resources with role demands*

Role in the Family Domain	Role Demands (A)	Role Resources (B)	Surplus versus Deficit	Role Priority	Resource Allocation Given Role Priority
Mother	7	7	0	9	Maintain
Wife	4	4	0	9	Maintain
Chauffeur	6	3	-3	6	Increase (priority = 2)
Cook	4	3	-1	5	Increase (priority = 3)
Shopper	8	2	-4	7	Increase (priority = 1)
Accountant	4	4	0	9	Maintain
PTA member	3	3	0	6	Maintain
President of the HOA	3	3	0	3	Maintain
Social events coordinator	5	5	0	1	Maintain

Notes:

• **Role Demands** (the extent to which the person perceives the time, energy, and other resources required to perform this role successfully); this can be measured using the following 10-point rating scale: from "1 = This Role Requires Very Low Amounts of Time, Energy, and Other Resources to Perform Successfully" to "10 = This Role Requires Very High Amounts of Time, Energy, and Other Resources to Perform Successfully"

• **Role Resources** (the extent to which the person has the resources needed to meet the demands of the role in question); this can be measured using the following 10-point rating scale: from "1 = I Do Not Have the Required Time, Energy, and Other Resources to Perform This Role Successfully" to "10 = I Do Have the Required Time, Energy, and Other Resources to Perform this Role Successfully"

• **Surplus versus Deficit:** Surplus occurs when role resources exceed role demands and deficit occurs when role resources fall below role demands; this can be computed by a simple difference algorithm: (A − B)

• **Role Priorities:** the extent to which the person perceives the specific role to be important in life ("1 = Least Important"; "10 = Extremely Important")

Table 7.3 *Managing your role conflict by matching role resources with role demands*

Role in the .... Domain	Role Demands (A)	Role Resources (B)	Surplus versus Deficit	Role Priority	Resource Allocation Given Role Priority
Role 1:	...	...	...		
Role 2:	...	...	...		
Role 3:	...	...	...		
Role 4:	...	...	...		
Role 5:	...	...	...		
Role 6:	...	...	...		
Role 7:	...	...	...		
Role 8:	...	...	...		
Role 9:	...	...	...		

Notes:
- **Role Demands** (the extent to which the person perceives the time, energy, and other resources required to perform this role successfully); this can be measured using the following 10-point rating scale: from "1 = This Role Requires Very Low Amounts of Time, Energy, and Other Resources to Perform Successfully" to "10 = This Role Requires Very High Amounts of Time, Energy, and Other Resources to Perform Successfully"
- **Role Resources** (the extent to which the person has the resources needed to meet the demands of the role in question); this can be measured using the following 10-point rating scale: from "1 = I Do Not Have the Required Time, Energy, and Other Resources to Perform This Role Successfully" to "10 = I Do Have the Required Time, Energy, and Other Resources to Perform This Role Successfully"
- **Surplus versus Deficit:** Surplus occurs when role resources exceed role demands and deficit occurs when role resources fall below role demands; this can be computed by a simple difference algorithm: (A − B)
- **Role Priorities**: the extent to which the person perceives the specific role to be important in life ("1 = Least Important"; "10 = Extremely Important")

She has just decided that she has to change her time management lifestyle. To do this, she has to work hard to form positive habits related to time management. As such, she created a timetable to monitor her time management habits for the next several months (see Table 7.4). She posted her time management table on the door of her fridge in the kitchen to ensure that she sees it around dinner time every evening. The goal is to answer "yes" or "no" for every time management question on the table and to do this every evening for the next two to three months. The end goal is to form a time management *habit*.

Answering the questions in the timetable shown in Table 7.4 helped Daniella form a time management habit that over time became part of her lifestyle. The instructor can use a similar table (see Table 7.5) as a template

Table 7.4 *Daniella's attempt to get into the habit of effective time management*

Daily Action	Day 1	Day 2	Day 3	Day 4	Day 5	Day 6	Day 7
Did I use the mobile phone calendar (and only that calendar) to schedule meetings and events *today*?	Yes	Yes	Yes	Yes	Yes	Yes	Yes
Did I remember to carry my mobile phone with me at all times *today*?	No	No	No	Yes	Yes	Yes	Yes
Did I make sure to charge my mobile phone *today*?	Yes	No	No	No	No	Yes	Yes
Did I mark all committed meetings and events *today*?	Yes	No	Yes	No	Yes	Yes	Yes
Did I check the calendar before making future commitments *today*?	No	No	No	No	No	Yes	Yes
Did I use the meeting alarm notification for every event and meeting *today*?	No	No	No	Yes	Yes	Yes	Yes
Did I check my calendar first thing in the morning *today*?	Yes	No	Yes	Yes	Yes	Yes	yes
Did I coordinate the scheduling of meetings and events with significant others *today*?	No	No	No	No	Yes	No	Yes
Did I attend all scheduled meetings and events *today*?	No	No	Yes	Yes	Yes	Yes	yes

to encourage the workshop participants to monitor their actions concerning time management and to take future corrective action.

Stress management is also another umbrella of interventions designed to reduce stress stemming from role conflict. Among the popular stress management techniques are:

- Regular exercise (e.g., running, swimming, dancing, cycling, and aerobics)
- Quality sleep (e.g., set a sleep schedule, don't look at electronics before bed, try meditation or other forms of relaxation before bedtime)
- Relaxation techniques (e.g., yoga, meditation, deep breathing, biofeedback, connecting with people, and laugh therapy)

Of course, these stress management techniques could not be practiced in the context of the workshop/seminar. Instead, the instructor may discuss these

Table 7.5 *A timetable template to monitor one's time management-related actions*

Daily Action	Day 1	Day 2	Day 3	Day 4	Day 5	Day 6	Day 7
Did I use the mobile phone calendar (and only that calendar) to schedule meetings and events *today*?							
Did I remember to carry my mobile phone with me at all times *today*?							
Did I make sure to charge my mobile phone *today*?							
Did I mark all committed meetings and events *today*?							
Did I check the calendar before making future commitments *today*?							
Did I use the meeting alarm notification for every event and meeting *today*?							
Did I check my calendar first thing in the morning *today*?							
Did I coordinate the scheduling of meetings and events with significant others *today*?							
Did I attend all scheduled meetings and events *today*?							

techniques with particular reference to role conflict and how these techniques can reduce stress from role conflict with specific and personal anecdotes.

7.3 Conclusion

In this chapter, we discussed managing role conflict to help achieve work-life balance. Role conflict occurs when an employee fails to meet demand in nonwork life domains because of role engagement in work life, and vice versa. When employees manage role demand in multiple domains, they are less likely to experience psychological stress and role overload. Doing so helps guard against decreases in overall life satisfaction. Common interventions deemed successful include matching role demand with role resources, managing time, and managing stress. Matching role demand with role resources involves the reduction of role demand in roles that lack adequate resources or increasing role resources to meet role demand. Managing time involves the use of time management techniques such as downloading a calendar app on a mobile phone, marking all committed events on the calendar, checking the calendar before making future commitments, and using the phone alarm to provide alerts about impending events. Finally, managing stress involves the use of stress management techniques such as regular exercise, meditation and praying, and social support.

References

Achour, M., Grine, F., & Mohd Nor, M. R. (2014). Work-family conflict and coping strategies: Qualitative study of Muslim female academicians in Malaysia. *Mental Health, Religion, & Culture*, 17(10), 1002–1014.

Adams, G. A. & Jex, S. M. (1999). Relationships between time management, control, work–family conflict, and strain. *Journal of Occupational Health Psychology*, 4(1), 72–77.

Allen, T. D. (2001). Family-supportive work environments: The role of organizational perceptions. *Journal of Vocational Behavior*, 58(3), 414–435.

Allen, T. D. & Armstrong, J. (2006). Further examination of the link between work-family conflict and physical health: The role of health-related behaviors. *American Behavioral Scientist*, 49(9), 1204–1221.

Ayman, R. & Antani, A. (2008). Social support and work–family conflict. In K. Korabik, D. S. Lero, & D. L. Whitehead (Eds.), *Handbook of work-family integration: Research, theory and best practices* (pp. 287–304). Amsterdam: Elsevier.

Byron, K. (2005). A meta-analytic review of work–family conflict and its antecedents. *Journal of Vocational Behavior*, 67(2), 169–198.

Carlson, D. S., Kacmar, K. M., & Williams, L. J. (2000). Construction and initial validation of a multidimensional measure of work–family conflict. *Journal of Vocational Behavior*, 56(2), 249–276.

Clayton, R. W., Thomas, C. H., Singh, B., & Winkel, D. E. (2015). Exercise as a means of reducing perceptions of work-family conflict: A test of the roles of self-efficacy and psychological strain. *Human Resource Management*, 54(6), 1013–1035.

DeGroot, T. & Kiker, D. S. (2003). A meta-analysis of the non-monetary effects of employee health management programs. *Human Resource Management*, 42(1), 53–69.

Drummond, S., O'Driscoll, M. P., Brough, P. et al. (2017). The relationship of social support with well-being outcomes via work-family conflict: Moderating effects of gender, dependents and nationality. *Human Relations*, 70(5), 544–565.

Edwards, J. R. & Rothbard, N. P. (2000). Mechanisms linking work and family: Clarifying the relationship between work and family constructs. *Academy of Management Review*, 25(1), 178–199.

Epstein, C. F. & Kalleberg, A. L. (2004). *Fighting for time: Shifting boundaries of work and social life*. New York: Russell Sage Foundation.

Fisher, G. G., Bulger, C. A., & Smith, C. S. (2009). Beyond work and family: a measure of work/nonwork interference and enhancement. *Journal of Occupational Health Psychology*, 14(4), 441–455.

Friedman, S. D., & Greenhaus, J. H. (2000). *Work and family – allies or enemies? What happens when business professionals confront life choices.* Oxford: Oxford University Press, USA.

Frone, M. R. (2003). Work-family balance. In J. C. Quick & L. E. Tetrick (Eds.), *Handbook of occupational health psychology* (pp. 143–162). Washington, DC: American Psychological Association.

Frone, M. R., Russell, M., & Cooper, M. L. (1992). Antecedents and outcomes of work-family conflict: testing a model of the work-family interface. *Journal of Applied Psychology*, 77(1), 65–83.

Frone, M. R., J. K. Yardley, and K. S. Markel (1997). Developing and testing an integrative model of the work–family interface. *Journal of Vocational Behavior*, 50(2), 145–167.

Grace, S. L., Williams, A., Stewart, D. E., & Franche, R. L. (2006). Health-promoting behaviors through pregnancy, maternity leave, and return to work: Effects of role spillover and other correlates. *Women & Health*, 43(2), 51–72.

Grandey, A. A. & Cropanzano, R. (1999). The conservation of resources model applied to work–family conflict and strain. *Journal of Vocational Behavior*, 54(2), 350–370.

Green, P. & Skinner, D. (2005). Does time management training work? An evaluation. *International Journal of Training and Development*, 9(2), 124–139.

Greenhaus, J. H., & Beutell, N. J. (1985). Sources of conflict between work and family roles. *Academy of Management Review*, 10(1), 76–88.

Grzywacz, J. G. & Marks, N. F. (2001). Social inequalities and exercise during adulthood: Toward an ecological perspective. *Journal of Health and Social Behavior*, 42(2), 202–220.

Hobfoll, S. E. (1989). Conservation of resources: a new attempt at conceptualizing stress. *American Psychologist*, 44(3), 513–524.

Kiburz, K. M., Allen, T. D., & French, K. A. (2017). Work-family conflict and mindfulness: Investigating the effectiveness of a brief training intervention. *Journal of Organizational Behavior*, 38(7), 1016–1037.

Kossek, E. E., Ozeki, C., & Kosier, D. W. (2001). Wellness incentives: Lessons learned about organizational change. *Human Resource Planning*, 24(4), 24–35.

Leiter, M. P. & Maslach, C. (2005). *Banishing burnout: Six strategies for improving your relationship with work.* New York: John Wiley & Sons.

Macan, T., Shahani, C., Dipboye, R. L., & Phillips, A. P. (1990). College students' time management: Correlations with academic performance and stress. *Journal of Educational Psychology*, 82(4), 760–768

Neck, C. P. & Cooper, K. H. (2000). The fit executive: Exercise and diet guidelines for enhancing performance. *Academy of Management Executive*, 14(2), 72–83.

Netemeyer, R. G., Boles, J. S., & McMurrian, R. (1996). Development and validation of work–family conflict and family–work conflict scales. *Journal of Applied Psychology*, 81(4), 400–410.

O'Driscoll, M. & Brough, P. (2010). Work organisation and health. In S. Leka & J. Houdmont (Eds.), *Occupational health psychology* (pp. 57–87). Chichester: Wiley-Blackwell.

Parasuraman, S., Greenhaus, J. H., & Granrose, C. S. (1992). Role stressors, social support, and well-being among two-career couples. *Journal of Organizational Behavior*, 13(4), 339–356.

Parks, K. M. & Steelman, L. A. (2008). Organizational wellness programs: A meta-analysis. *Journal of Occupational Health Psychology*, 13(1), 58–68.

Rau, B. L. & Hyland, M. A. M. (2002). Role conflict and flexible work arrangements: The effects on applicant attraction. *Personnel Psychology*, 55(1), 111–136.

Roos, E., Sarlio-Lähteenkorva, S., Lallukka, T., & Lahelma, E. (2007). Associations of work-family conflicts with food habits and physical activity. *Public Health Nutrition*, 10(3), 222–229.

Sturges, J. & Guest, D. (2004). Working to live or living to work? Work/life balance early in the career. *Human Resource Management Journal*, 14(4), 5–20.

Voydanoff, P. (2005). Consequences of boundary-spanning demands and resources for work-to-family conflict and perceived stress. *Journal of Occupational Health Psychology*, 10(4), 491–505.

CHAPTER 8

Creating Role Balance

8.1 Creating Role Balance

When people engage in multiple roles, they are likely to experience satisfaction of growth needs (i.e., social, knowledge, aesthetics, self-actualization, and self-transcendence needs) as well as satisfaction of basic needs (i.e., health, safety, and economic needs). Satisfaction of both sets of basic and growth needs contributes significantly and positively to life satisfaction (e.g., Alderfer, 1972; Herzberg, 1966; Maslow, 1954, 1970; Matuska, 2012; Sheldon, Cummins, & Kamble, 2010; Sheldon & Niemiec, 2006). For example, Matuska (2012) conceptualized role balance as congruence between both desired and actual time spent in activities related to a specific role that satisfies basic and growth needs (needs related to health, relationship, challenge/interest, and identity). The author conducted a study that successfully demonstrated a strong association between role balance and personal wellbeing.

As such, role balance involves engaging in balanced activities – balanced between activities designed to maintain role functioning (maintenance activities related to basic needs) and activities designed to allow the individual to flourish in that role (flourishing activities related to growth needs). That is, life satisfaction is a derivative of role balance – the extent to which work and nonwork roles serve to meet both basic plus growth needs. Meeting basic needs serves to maintain the biological and psychological integrity of the individual. Failure to meet basic needs results in dissatisfaction; and if dissatisfaction accumulates across work and nonwork roles, this dissatisfaction turns into life dissatisfaction. Conversely, meeting growth needs allows the individual to flourish – cognitively, emotionally, and socially. Failure to meet growth needs results in a lack of satisfaction, which is different from dissatisfaction. Aggregate satisfaction across work and nonwork roles contributes significantly to life satisfaction. That is, basic needs are more closely related to dissatisfaction than satisfaction; and conversely, growth needs are more closely related to satisfaction than dissatisfaction. This is the essence of Herzberg's (1966) two-factor theory in industrial/organizational psychology.

People engage in maintenance activities in work and nonwork roles to meet basic needs. We use the term "maintenance activities" because these activities are necessary for the individual to function in daily life. We need to function on a daily basis, and we need to function reasonably well to be able to flourish. "Flourishing activities" in work and nonwork roles serve to meet growth needs. As such, role balance is created by engaging in both maintenance and flourishing activities in work and nonwork roles.

So, what are some maintenance and flourishing activities that are essential to creating role balance? To reiterate, maintenance activities tend to satisfy basic needs, not growth needs. Conversely, flourishing activities involve activities designed to satisfy growth needs. We will discuss maintenance versus flourishing activities by focusing on work and nonwork domains.

8.1.1 Creating Role Balance in Work Life: Maintenance Plus Flourishing Activities

Do you work to live, or do you live to work? Many industrial/organizational psychologists have long asked this question and answered it with a resounding answer: *both*. In other words, we work to make a living – to make an income that supports our way of living. We work to meet our basic needs – food security, housing and shelter, health and safety, economic needs, etc. We also work because we are wired to work. Not working is against our human nature. Through work, our many growth needs – social needs, esteem needs, need for self-actualization, need for knowledge, and aesthetics and creativity needs – are met.

This distinction is made clear when you ask yourself whether your job is just a job or a fulfilling career. If it is just a job, then your work life is mostly about maintenance – your job allows you to maintain a lifestyle that you are accustomed to. As such, you must engage in work to make a decent living, the kind of income that can support your basic needs and possibly your economic needs. However, a job as a career is much more. It goes beyond maintenance. It is about flourishing. The goal of working just to make money is not likely to be fulfilling. Work, for most people who identify themselves as having a "career," provides them with the opportunity to set for themselves important lifelong goals and to strive to meet these goals. Monitoring goal progress and anticipating goal attainment is key to positive emotions related to achievement, pride, hope, optimism, esteem, meaning, purpose, self-determination, competence, autonomy, and internal locus of control. Knowing this, it is important to develop a career and make strides toward career development.

Much of the research literature on work motivation in industrial/organizational psychology makes a distinction between intrinsic and extrinsic motivation (Amabile, 1993), which can be viewed in terms of the traditional distinction between low-order (basic) and high-order (growth) needs (Maslow, 1962). A person who is motivated to do a job because it is a job that provides them a paycheck and other fringe benefits is extrinsically motivated. As such, the job serves to satisfy mostly low-order (basic) rather than high-order (growth) needs. Conversely, a job considered to be a career involves intrinsic motivation – the job satisfies high-order (growth) needs. Low-order needs are essential needs related to survival: biological needs (needs for food, water, air, sex, etc.), health and safety needs, economic needs, and ultimately the minimum financial resources for the sustenance of oneself (and possibly one's family). At their most basic level, they are needs related to survival and the propagation of the human species. Satisfying basic needs involves "maintenance" activities in work life. In contrast, high-order needs are growth-related. They include a wide assortment of needs such as social and relatedness needs, esteem and effectance (perception of agency or control of one's environment) needs, self-actualization needs, needs related to aesthetics and creativity, and intellectual and autonomy needs, among others. Many of these human needs are met through career development. Satisfying growth needs involves "flourishing" activities in work life.

Research (e.g., Herzberg, 1974; Sanjeev & Surya, 2016) has demonstrated that a job that fails to meet basic needs causes substantial job dissatisfaction (negative feelings and emotions such as anger, fear, anxiety, despair, hopelessness, and depression). However, a job that meets basic needs does not contribute much to job satisfaction or positive emotions (e.g., happiness and joy). A good job that meets basic needs can provide only relief, not joy or happiness. Conversely, a job that satisfies high-order needs can contribute significantly to positive emotions such as happiness. A job that fails to meet high-order needs but still satisfies basic needs is not likely to cause much job dissatisfaction.

Let's provide the reader with an example. This case involves John, a professor of mathematics. Most of his colleagues who knew him well have described him as having an imbalanced life. He devoted more than 90 percent of his work time to research and writing – specifically research and writing designed to produce publications. Being at a research university, research and writing are imperative. Faculty at research universities take to heart the adage: "publish or perish." John was also highly motivated to engage in research because it satisfied his "growth needs" – the need for esteem, self-actualization, knowledge, and creativity. The problem was that he was sloppy. His office was a mess. He would have a hard time finding reports, books, and research materials. Luckily, he had at least two graduate assistants and a secretary who helped. Thus, maintenance tasks (such as organizing files, developing PowerPoint slides, typing reports and manuscripts, making travel arrangements, and servicing his computer and other multimedia gadgets) were someone else's responsibility – never his. Even his contact list on his phone was not his responsibility. Unfortunately for John, modern technology has displaced graduate assistants and secretaries. In the modern landscape of today's universities, graduate assistants are not often assigned "gofer-like duties." University administration expects faculty to involve their graduate students with their own research leading to publications. That is, graduate students become, in essence, research interns working on research projects that eventually lead to publication, where they are acknowledged for their research input. Secretaries also no longer perform "secretarial duties" in the traditional sense. They no longer support faculty by typing their manuscripts and making travel arrangements. Their positions have transformed into technical specialties such as financial accounting, inventory and logistics, and research compliance, among others.

Going back to John, the "maintenance" support he once enjoyed is now no longer available. His passion for focusing on research and writing has been hampered by his own chaotic lifestyle. His scholarly productivity plummeted, and he refused to adjust to the rapidly evolving landscape of research universities. He became frustrated and angry at every turn. He complained constantly; the world around him kept crashing down. Most other university faculty learned to adjust by assuming new roles that were once relegated to graduate assistants and secretaries. They learned how to use information technology to get things done efficiently. Thus, successful faculty who engage in "flourishing" activities such as research and writing also have to do "housekeeping" (i.e., maintenance activities). Housekeeping duties are required to allow faculty to prosper in a research university environment.

As such, to create role balance, we all need to engage in both maintenance and flourishing activities in our work life.

8.1.2   Creating Role Balance in Nonwork Life: Maintenance Plus Flourishing Activities

Nonwork life involves several life domains such as family life, health and safety, love life, financial life, social life, leisure life, and cultural life. We will focus on *family life* as a representative domain of nonwork life.

Family life extends beyond the household. Family life often involves a combination of children, parents, siblings, and possibly other close relatives. Family structure tends to be different for singles, divorced, and widowed; as such, family members are likely to be defined differently in these households. Maintaining good relationships with family members is very important to personal happiness. For those who are divorced, maintaining a good relationship with one's ex is equally important. Maintaining a good relationship with family members requires significant time, effort, and often money. This includes aspects such as childcare, schooling, meal preparation, attending to the sick, elderly care, household chores, and shopping for family needs, among a multitude of other essential tasks.

Flourishing in family life entails activities designed to inject excitement into the family routine. Examples include planning a family vacation (or a family reunion), holding social events with family members, engaging in sports or activities with family members, and engaging in leisure activities with family members, and making meal preparation a social event where each family member participates.

Consider the following seminal study conducted by Professor Christopher Ellison (1990). Using data from the National Survey of Black Americans, the study investigated relationships between kinship bonds and subjective wellbeing. The study found that subjective family closeness is a strong predictor of personal happiness among all Black individuals, and the same construct (subjective family closeness) is a strong predictor of life satisfaction among older Black adults only. There is substantial research in the wellbeing literature suggesting that personal happiness is a lower form of subjective wellbeing directly related to positive and negative affect; whereas, life satisfaction is a higher form (Sirgy, 2019, 2020). Lower forms of subjective wellbeing can be construed as directly related to maintenance activities, whereas higher forms of subjective wellbeing are more related to flourishing activities. As such, the finding that subjective family closeness is a strong predictor of life satisfaction among older Black adults is not surprising given that life satisfaction is related to "flourishing" activities.

Consider the case of Robert, a building contractor. He was recently divorced. He and his ex-wife, Mindy, have four children ages 4 to 14. He is now sharing custody – 30/70 (i.e., 30 percent with him and 70 percent with her). Robert is conservative in both his political and social views, and he always relegated home duties and housekeeping to Mindy. He moved out of their home after the divorce and rented an apartment close by. Recently, his friend, Jamie, visited him and commented that his apartment looked so messy – he has yet to fully unpack, needs to buy more furniture, there are clothes everywhere, dishes in the sink, and the place was quite dirty. He has yet to cook a meal at the apartment; he has been eating out all the time; and when the children come to visit, he also takes them out – spending a little fortune at nearby restaurants. He thought he could afford it given the fact that his contracting business is thriving. Additionally, he has been spoiling his children by taking them shopping, has been buying them all kinds of video games, and has enjoyed playing with them – he even set up an elaborate play station in his apartment.

However, the kids have been complaining lately because his apartment is a mess. They don't want to spend time in the filthy environment, let alone stay overnight. His friends are complaining too – they have been inviting him to their place with no reciprocity, and they're getting tired of it. Furthermore, he has been late showing up to appointments and in some instances missed them entirely. He can't leave the apartment on time to make these appointments because his place is so disorganized – a simple example is misplacing his car keys; it takes him an inordinate amount of time to find his keys every morning making him late for his appointments.

Jamie, his good friend, asked him a few weeks ago whether he is happier given the divorce. His answer was "yes, initially but no, not now." In a nutshell, his *lack of maintenance* in his family life is now causing problems in other aspects of his life (from family life, social life, to work life). In other words, Robert has a *role imbalance problem* in his family life causing negative spillover and reducing his life satisfaction overall.

What should he do? Jamie suggested that he needs a housekeeper, and he knows of an older woman who might be a perfect candidate for him. The housekeeper, Gloria, is a woman in her sixties who is between jobs; the family she had been working for moved to another state. Robert interviewed Gloria and was very impressed with her references; he hired her on the spot. Gloria was heaven-sent. His apartment is now impeccably clean, everything is well-organized, and most importantly Gloria has been cooking wonderful meals that the kids love. He invited Jamie and his wife for dinner, and Jamie was very impressed. He gave him the thumbs up.

Robert has managed to restore balance in his family life – balance between maintenance and flourishing activities. Doing so served to reverse the downward (negative) spiral; he is now experiencing an upward (positive) spiral because he managed to "get his house in order."

8.2 Developing a Training Program Guided by the Principle of Role Balance

Role imbalance occurs when the individual fails to balance maintenance and flourishing activities in performing a specific work or nonwork role. To perform successfully, both sets of activities have to be accomplished. Table 8.1 shows example maintenance and flourishing activities broken down by life domain.

The instructor of the work-life balance workshop could present this table to the workshop participants and would discuss examples of maintenance and flourishing activities within each of the work and nonwork domains.

After describing the maintenance and flourishing activities commonly used to achieve role balance, the instructor can present a template table (Table 8.2) and encourage the workshop participants to complete this table

Table 8.1 *Maintenance and flourishing strategies commonly used in work and nonwork life domains*

Life Domain	Maintenance and Flourishing Activities
Work life	*Maintenance strategies*: Arrive or begin work on time every day, avoid excessive absences, and perform your required job duties in a timely manner
	Flourishing strategies: Set career goals. Develop concrete plans to attain career goals. Monitor progress toward goal attainment.
Nonwork life (health and safety)	*Maintenance strategies*: Maintain a healthy lifestyle through physical exercise and eating a well-balanced diet. Have regular health checkups and comply with doctors' orders
	Flourishing strategies: Make physical exercise a sport. Make cooking a hobby. Plan social outings with nutritious meals and physical exercise.
Nonwork life (marital affairs)	*Maintenance strategies*: Make plans to maintain your relationship with your romantic partner, such as getting married or buying a house together
	Flourishing strategies: Take your spouse out for a romantic dinner. Get together with good friends as a couple. Travel with your significant other. Reminisce about the positive experiences you have shared as a couple. Keep your sex life active and exciting.

Table 8.1 *(cont.)*

Life Domain	Maintenance and Flourishing Activities
Nonwork life (family affairs)	*Maintenance strategies*: Maintaining a good relationship with family members requires significant time, effort, and often money. This may include childcare, schooling, meal preparation, attending to the sick, elderly care, doing household chores, and shopping for family needs, among a multitude of other essential tasks. *Flourishing strategies*: Flourishing entails injecting fun and passion into the family routine. Examples include planning a family vacation, holding social events with family members, engaging in sports with family members, and engaging in leisure activities with family members.
Nonwork life (financial affairs)	*Maintenance strategies*: Perform a job that produces enough income to pay the bills and buy the essentials. *Flourishing strategies*: Invest for future growth. Consume goods and services that have elements of novelty and excitement.
Nonwork life (social relationships)	*Maintenance strategies*: Attend important family functions such as weddings as well as funerals. Support relatives and friends when they are sick or are in need. Attend social events at work to strengthen the social bond with your coworkers. *Flourishing strategies*: Play an exciting game with your friends on a regular basis. Go out with friends on a social outing – dinner and movie. Join a social club that meets regularly.
Nonwork life (leisure and recreation)	*Maintenance strategies*: Engage in leisure activities that can help you relax and de-stress. *Flourishing strategies*: Engage in competitive games that allow you to express related skills and mastery. Start a new hobby that you enjoy.
Nonwork life (travel and cultural affairs)	*Maintenance strategies*: Engage in cultural activities to learn about your own culture and the culture of other people in other places. The goal is to enjoy the pleasures of traveling. *Flourishing strategies*: Travel to destinations that reflect aspects of your own personal identity, spirituality, and heritage. Travel to destinations to learn about the cultures of other people to expand your knowledge and wisdom.

on their own. The goal is to prompt the participants to document their maintenance and flourishing activities within each work and nonwork domain. Doing so should allow them to assess the extent of role balance they currently experience in those domains and, if necessary, how to act to restore role balance. The instructor could also encourage the workshop participants to share their stories characterizing role imbalance and how they can increase work-life balance by restoring the noted role imbalances.

Table 8.2 *Applying the role balance principle in work and nonwork domains to increase work–life balance*

Life Domain	Maintenance Strategies and Role Satisfaction (A)	Flourishing Strategies and Role Satisfaction (B)	Satisfaction Difference (A–B)
Work life	Examples include arriving or beginning work on time every day, avoiding excessive absences, and performing your required job duties in a timely manner Satisfaction A =	Examples include setting career goals, developing concrete plans to attain career goals, and monitoring progress toward goal attainment Satisfaction B=	...
Health and safety Life	Examples include maintaining a healthy lifestyle through physical exercise and eating a well-balanced diet, having regular health checkups, and complying with doctors' orders Satisfaction A =	Examples include making physical exercise a sport, making cooking a hobby, and planning social outings with nutritious meals and physical exercise Satisfaction B =	...
Marital life	Examples include making plans to maintain your relationship with your romantic partner, such as getting married or buying a house together Satisfaction A =	Examples include taking your spouse out for a romantic dinner, getting together with good friends as a couple, traveling with your significant other, reminiscing about positive experiences you shared as a couple, and keeping your sex life active and exciting, Satisfaction B =	...
Family life	Maintaining a good relationship with family members requires significant time, effort, and often money (e.g., childcare, schooling, meal preparation, attending to the sick, elderly care, doing household chores, shopping for family needs, among a multitude of other essential tasks) Satisfaction A =	Flourishing entails injecting fun and passion into the family routine (e.g., planning a family vacation, holding social events with family members, engaging in sports with family members, engaging in leisure activities with family members). Satisfaction B =	...

Life domain	Maintenance Activities	Flourishing Activities	
Financial life	Examples include performing a job that produces enough income to pay the bills and buy the essentials Satisfaction A =	Examples include investing for future growth and consuming goods and services that have elements of novelty and excitement. Satisfaction B =	⋮
Social life	Examples include attending important family functions such as weddings as well as funerals, supporting relatives and friends when they are sick or are in need, and attending social events at work to strengthen the social bond with your co-workers Satisfaction A =	Examples include playing an exciting game with your friends on a regular basis, going out with friends on a social outing (e.g., dinner and movie), and joining a social club that meets regularly. Satisfaction B =	⋮
Leisure life	Examples include engaging in leisure activities that can help you relax and de-stress Satisfaction A =	Examples include engaging in competitive games that allow you to express related skills and mastery, and starting a new hobby that you enjoy. Satisfaction B =	⋮
Travel and cultural life	Examples include engaging in cultural activities to learn about your own culture and the culture of other people in other places Satisfaction A =	Examples include traveling to destinations that reflect aspects of your own personal identity, spirituality, and heritage; and traveling to destinations to learn about the cultures of other people to expand your knowledge and wisdom. Satisfaction B =	⋮

Notes:

- **Satisfaction with Maintenance Activities:** Responses can be captured on a 10-point rating scale: "1 = Very Dissatisfied"; "10 = Very Satisfied"
- **Satisfaction with Flourishing Activities:** Responses can be captured on a 10-point rating scale: "1 = Very Dissatisfied"; "10 = Very Satisfied"
- **Satisfaction Difference:** Arithmetic difference between Satisfaction with Maintenance Flourishing Activities

8.3   Conclusion

In this chapter we discussed a behavior-based intervention we referred to as role balance. Role balance involves engaging in balanced activities – balanced between activities designed to maintain role functioning (maintenance activities related to basic needs) and activities designed to allow the individual to flourish in that role (flourishing activities related to growth needs). We argued that life satisfaction is influenced by the extent to which work and nonwork roles serve to meet both basic and growth needs. Meeting basic needs serves to maintain the biological and psychological integrity of the individual. Failure to meet basic needs results in dissatisfaction; and if dissatisfaction accumulates across work and nonwork roles, this dissatisfaction turns into life dissatisfaction. Conversely, meeting growth needs allows the individual to flourish, emotionally and socially. Failure to meet growth needs results in a lack of satisfaction, which is different from dissatisfaction. Aggregate satisfaction across work and nonwork roles contributes significantly to life satisfaction.

As such, people engage in maintenance activities in work and nonwork roles to meet basic needs. Flourishing activities in work and nonwork roles serve to meet growth needs. In that vein, role balance is created by engaging in both maintenance and flourishing activities in work and nonwork roles.

We then described some maintenance and flourishing activities that are essential to creating role balance in work and nonwork domains. Concerning the work domain, we argued that a job that fails to meet basic needs causes substantial job dissatisfaction (negative feelings and emotions such as anger, fear, anxiety, despair, hopelessness, and depression). By the same token, a job that meets basic needs does not contribute much to job satisfaction or positive emotions (e.g., happiness and joy). A good job that meets basic needs can provide only relief, not joy or happiness. Conversely, a job that satisfies growth needs can contribute significantly to positive emotions such as happiness. A job that fails to meet high-order needs but still satisfies basic needs is not likely to cause much job dissatisfaction. As such, to create role balance, we all need to engage in both maintenance and flourishing activities in our work life.

Concerning nonwork life, we described maintenance and flourishing activities in family life. We used family life as a representative domain of nonwork life. Other domains include health and safety, love life, financial life, social life, leisure life, and cultural life. Maintaining good relationships with family members is also very important to personal happiness.

Maintaining a good relationship with family members requires significant time, effort, and often money. This includes aspects such as childcare, schooling, meal preparation, attending to the sick, elderly care, household chores, and shopping for family needs, among a multitude of other essential tasks. In contrast, flourishing in family life entails injecting excitement into the family routine. Examples include planning a family vacation (or a family reunion), holding social events with family members, engaging in sports or activities with family members, engaging in leisure activities with family members, and making meal preparation a social event where each family member participates. To create role balance in family life, people have to engage in both maintenance and flourishing activities in that domain.

We then discussed how instructors of work-life balance programs can implement the role balance principle in workshops designed to train employees on how to increase work-life balance. This training involves explaining to the workshop participants how people commonly use maintenance and flourishing activities to create role balance in every aspect of their work and nonwork domains.

The five personal interventions discussed in this chapter are essentially behavior-based. That is, they are personal interventions characterized by action or behavior. This is why we referred to them as "behavior-based" personal interventions. In the next chapter, we will continue discussing personal interventions for work-life balance, but the focus will be on "cognition-based interventions." That is, the personal interventions require a change in the employee's mental state. These interventions include positive spillover, segmentation, value-based compensation, and whole-life perspective.

References

Alderfer, C. P. (1972). *Existence, relatedness, and growth: Human needs in organizational settings*. New York: The Free Press.

Amabile, T. M. (1993). Motivational synergy: Toward new conceptualizations of intrinsic and extrinsic motivation in the workplace. *Human Resource Management Review*, 3(3), 185–201.

Ellison, C. G. (1990). Family ties, friendships, and subjective well-being among Black Americans. *Journal of Marriage and the Family*, 52(2), 298–310.

Herzberg, F. (1966). *Work and the nature of man*. Cleveland: World.

Herzberg, F. (1974). The wise and old Turk. *Harvard Business Review*, 52(5), 70–80.

Maslow, A. H. (1954, 1970). *Motivation and personality*. New York: Harper.

Maslow, A. (1962). *Toward a psychology of being*. New York: Nostrand.

Matuska, K. (2012). Validity evidence of a model and measure of life balance. *Occupation, Participation and Health*, 32(1), 229–237.

Sanjeev, M. A. & Surya, A. V. (2016). Two factor theory of motivation and satisfaction: An empirical verification. *Annals of Data Science*, 3(2), 155–173.

Sheldon, K. M., Cummins, R., & Kamble, S. (2010). Life balance and well-being: Testing a novel conceptual and measurement approach. *Journal of Personality*, 78(4), 1093–1134.

Sheldon, K. M. & Niemiec, C. P. (2006). It's not just the amount that counts: Balanced need satisfaction also affects well-being. *Journal of Personality and Social Psychology*, 91(2), 331–341.

Sirgy, M. J. (2019). Positive balance: A hierarchical perspective of positive mental health. *Quality of Life Research*, 28(7), 1921–1930.

Sirgy, M. J. (2020). *Positive balance: A theory of well-being and positive mental health*. Cham, Switzerland: Springer Nature Switzerland AG.

Cognition-Based Personal Interventions of Work-Life Balance

In Part II of the book, we made the distinction between behavior-based personal interventions of work-life balance and cognition-based interventions. Part II was dedicated to behavior-based interventions. Part III of the book focuses on cognition-based personal interventions of work-life balance. These are:

- Chapter 9: Segmenting Roles and Domains
- Chapter 10: Integrating Roles and Domains
- Chapter 11: Engaging in Value-Based Compensation
- Chapter 12: Applying Whole-Life Perspective in Decision-Making

See Figure PIII.1 for a visual.

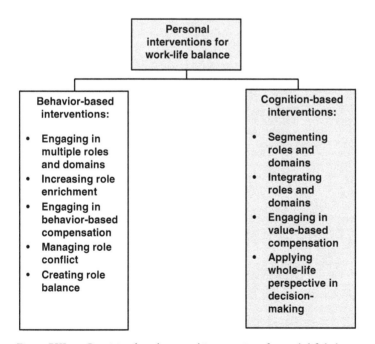

Figure PIII.1   Cognition-based personal interventions for work-life balance

A friendly reminder. As previously noted (in Part II of the book), the distinction between behavior-based personal interventions of work-life balance and cognition-based interventions is a matter of degree rather than a categorical difference. That is, behavior-based interventions are mostly interventions initiated by explicit behaviors. The converse applies to cognition-based interventions. That is, the focus of cognition-based interventions involves a mental process. That is not to say, the mental process does not involve some explicit behaviors. In many cases, cognition-based interventions are manifested in terms of explicit behaviors.

CHAPTER 9

Segmenting Roles and Domains

9.1   Segmenting Roles and Domains

Negative feelings do spill over from one role to the next, one domain to another. For example, an employee has a bad day at the office; she comes home in a sour mood and that mood lingers at home. Conversely, she may argue with her husband; this argument puts her in a sour mood; she goes to work in the same mood, and that mood influences how she feels about work. This is what psychologists refer to as *negative spillover*. People deal with negative spillover by erecting psychological boundaries to insulate those domains housing negative affect. As such, the boundaries or borders serve to prevent negative spillover. Doing so helps the individual maintain overall life satisfaction – by preventing overall life satisfaction from plummeting because of "emotional contagion."

According to the boundary theory of work-life balance (Kreiner, Hollensbe, & Sheep, 2009), employees tend to segment or integrate life domains depending on their life circumstances. Segmentation is useful for those who experience a great deal of negative affect; thus, segmentation serves to reduce negative spillover. This is accomplished by setting up impermeable role boundaries (Ashforth, Kreiner, & Fugate, 2000). Conversely, integration is used for those employees who experience considerable positive affect. Hence, integration serves to facilitate positive spillover. Integration occurs when the employee makes the boundary between work and nonwork roles permeable. Integration is commonly used in teleworking situations – working from home (Rau & Hyland, 2002). Recent research on the concept of segmentation has demonstrated that the increased use of mobile technologies blurs the boundaries between work and family, making segmentation difficult (Chesley, 2005; Park, Fritz, & Jex, 2011).

To reiterate, segmentation involves a cognitive separation of two life domains so that the two domains do not influence each other. That is, individuals employing this strategy strive to erect a barrier or psychological wall around the domain with high dissatisfaction, making the wall impermeable (e.g., Ashforth, Kreiner, & Fugate, 2000; Bulger, Matthews, & Hoffman, 2007; Clark, 2000; Edwards & Rothbard, 2000; Kreiner, Hollensbe, & Sheep, 2009; Sirgy, 2002; Sonnentag, 2012; Sonnentag et al., 2008). They actively separate nonwork life from work life by actively suppressing work-related thoughts and feelings, thus preventing these thoughts and feelings from disrupting home life. Doing so is an effective mental strategy to preserve life satisfaction – prevent life satisfaction from slippage. In other words, segmentation involves a psychological detachment from the dissatisfying life domain, which in turn helps to prevent spillover of negative affect, thus serving as a buffer for overall life satisfaction.

Consider the following scenario comparing two individuals (Belinda and Hannah) who are both experiencing dissatisfaction at work: –3 units of dissatisfaction on an 11-point scale varying from –5 (very dissatisfied) to +5 (very satisfied). However, Belinda and Hannah are satisfied with their family life (+3 units of satisfaction). Both are experiencing negative spillover of affect from work life to family life. That is, their dissatisfaction at work (–3 units of satisfaction) is influencing their mood at home, causing friction and stress in family life. Belinda decides to deal with the high dissatisfaction at work by compartmentalizing her work life to prevent future negative spillover of negative affect from work life to family life. To accomplish this, she decides that at home she will not think about work issues, talk about work, or engage in any work-related activities. By doing so, Belinda manages to maintain her high satisfaction in family life (+3). Hannah, on the other hand, does not segment and thus experiences decreased satisfaction in family life as a result of the negative spillover from work.

How do employees experiencing negative affect in one life domain prevent the spillover of this negative affect into other domains using segmentation? They can do so using (1) temporal segmentation (i.e., controlling time), (2) physical segmentation (i.e., manipulating physical boundaries), (3) behavior segmentation (i.e., negotiating boundaries), and (4) communicative segmentation (i.e., managing expectations) (Kreiner, Hollensbe, & Sheep, 2009). Let's discuss these personal interventions in more depth.

9.1.1   Temporal Segmentation

Temporal segmentation refers to segmentation involving time control (Kreiner, Hollensbe, & Sheep, 2009). In other words, one can segment work life from interference from family life (or vice versa) by making decisions and changes in one's daily calendar. For example, one can create an impermeable boundary around family life by deciding that after-work hours are exclusively reserved for family time. No time will be allotted to work-related tasks. Temporal segmentation allows the individual to extract satisfaction from the compartmentalized domain by allocating much more time and energy to activities in that domain and that domain alone. Doing so increases the individual's involvement and engagement in that domain, which in turn may result in higher levels of satisfaction in the domain (Beutell & Wittig-Berman, 1999; Myrie & Daly, 2009; Wegge et al., 2007).

Consider the case of Kathy. Kathy is the manager of a landscaping service, whose business has been picking up lately due to new clients. Kathy has met with the new clients and made promises she may not be able to keep. She is very nervous about missing the deadlines she committed to. The landscaping service employs seven landscaping designers. Recently, three of her designers contracted COVID-19, and they have been fighting for their lives in the local hospital. She feels that "all hell is breaking loose" at work. Clients are calling and demanding immediate attention; the families of the sick landscapers have been worried about their loved ones and expressed concerns about paycheck interruptions. Kathy also has a family with three kids of school age. COVID-19 has wreaked havoc on the school routine – her kids are mandated to stay home and attend classes remotely. This situation has created much more family demand resulting in a great deal of stress at home. As such, Kathy is experiencing tremendous stress in both work and family life involving a significant negative spillover between the two domains compounding the problem. The stress from work is spilling over to the homefront, and stress at home is spilling over and adversely affecting her job. As a result, Kathy is feeling very dissatisfied with her life. To deal with this negative spillover, she decided to deal with work-related issues only between the hours of 8:00 a.m. and 4:00 p.m.; that is, she will not attend to family matters during that time. By the same token, she will give her full time and attention to deal with her kids' school situation after 4:00 p.m. In other words, all work-related matters will be put on hold for the next day – she will not attend to any work-related headaches after 4:00 p.m. This is what we are referring to as "temporal segmentation."

9.1.2 Physical Segmentation

Recent research has found that the increased use of mobile technologies blurs the boundaries between work and family, making segmentation difficult (Chesley, 2005; Park, Fritz, & Jex, 2011; Schieman & Young, 2013). Today more than ever, we have easy access to work-related platforms, such as email, from our home and mobile devices. This access is designed to enhance our ability to work remotely. This is, of course, both good and bad. The bad thing about this enhanced work accessibility, or what some scholars call "24/7 availability," is the fact that it may generate additional stress in other life domains. Work access at home can add stress by allowing work to intrude upon family life. This is a good illustration of the challenges of physical segmentation in the modern workplace.

To further demonstrate, consider the following survey item capturing physical segmentation of family life: "When I'm physically at home, I try not to address work-related issues so I can focus on my family" (see Table 9.1). This item illustrates how people segment their family life from interference from work by making and implementing the decision to protect the family domain through a physical barrier – the physical home. That is, physical segmentation involves attempts to identify spatial boundaries and insulate the domain by decisions to engage in domain-related activities within those specified boundaries – the physical home becomes the boundary protecting family life (Kreiner, Hollensbe, & Sheep, 2009). Thus, the use of physical boundaries in segmenting a given domain allows the individual to focus and experience more satisfaction in that domain as well as be more psychologically engaged in that domain (Carlson, Ferguson, & Kacmar, 2016). As such, to implement physical segmentation, when you are physically at home, try not to address work-related issues so you can focus on your family. This means strict adherence to physical separation in the home itself – you should only engage in the work while in the home office or other designated workspace. You should become engaged in nonwork activities only when you are outside of that space.[1]

Going back to Kathy's case: she is stressed at work and at home, and there is quite a bit of negative spillover between the two domains. What to do? She decides to deal with work-related issues at work – that is, at the landscaping company facility. By the same token, she also decides that she will give her full time and attention to her children when she is physically

---

[1] The physical home versus office is a good example of physical segmentation. But for those who work from home, the same distinction can be used between a home office and the rest of the house (i.e., an individual should only work in the home office, and once they are outside of that room they do not work). And further, the same principle also applies to any designated space inside the home; individuals should never work in bed or on their couch as those spaces are in the family domain. If an employee does not have a home office, they should pick a specific spot in their home such as a certain chair, desk, or table that they work from exclusively.

Table 9.1 *Types of segmentation interventions*

Intervention	Description	References
Temporal segmentation	Segmentation by creating time boundaries: one can segment work life from interference from family life (or vice versa) by making decisions and changes in one's daily calendar.	Carlson, Ferguson, and Kacmar (2016)
Physical segmentation	Segmentation by physical boundaries: one can insulate a domain by decisions to engage in domain-related activities within specified boundaries that are spatial in nature (e.g., the physical space of home residence becomes the boundary protecting family life).	Carlson, Ferguson, and Kacmar (2016)
Behavior segmentation	Segmentation by behavior-based boundaries: an example may be the use of two email accounts to separate professional from personal life.	Carlson, Ferguson, and Kacmar (2016)
Communicative segmentation	Segmentation by managing communication boundaries with others: an example is to request supervisors and coworkers not to call at home to discuss job-related concerns during non-business hours.	Carlson, Ferguson, and Kacmar (2016)

at home. In other words, all work-related matters will be attended to when she is physically present at the landscaping facility, and only there. Once she steps out of the facility, she will allow herself to deal with nonwork-related matters such as her kids' school headaches. This is what we are referring to as "physical segmentation."

9.1.3 Behavior Segmentation

Consider the following survey item to capture behavior segmentation in the work domain: "While at work, I use technology to help keep family demands out of my work life." This item shows a specific behavior (e.g., the use of technology to allow the person to focus on work responsibilities and minimize possible interference from family demands (Kreiner, Hollensbe, & Sheep, 2009; Carlson, Ferguson, & Kacmar, 2016).

For example, screening calls (i.e., using caller ID), having a separate work and personal cellphone or computer, or using two separate calendars or email accounts allows individuals to manage their boundaries. Caller ID allows the individual to identify the caller; if the caller is from work, the individual may reject the call, thereby allowing them to be fully engaged in family life with little interference from work life. How about not answering your work email at home? Here the segmentation is not only based on the physical space of being at home but also on not responding to work-related communications, *period*. The result of behavioral segmentation is to ensure maximum satisfaction in the family domain (Golden & Geisler, 2007; Park, Fritz, & Jex, 2011). Given the prevalence of technology, behavior-based segmentation is extremely important in regulating work and family domain separation. The use of behavior segmentation that keeps family out of work should contribute to greater job satisfaction and job engagement; and similarly, keeping work out of family should contribute to greater family satisfaction and family engagement.

Going back to Kathy's situation (described in the two preceding sections), Kathy decides to prevent the negative spillover between work and home life by separating her email accounts. In the past, her work email was her only email account, and she used that work account for all of her personal emails. Hence, she applied for a new "Gmail" account at Google to process her personal, and only personal, emails. She did the same with her laptop. She went to BestBuy and bought a laptop computer that she can use for nonwork stuff. These behaviors serve to segment her work life from her home life.

9.1.4   Communicative Segmentation

Industrial/organizational psychologists studying work-life balance assert that work contact (i.e., communication with work colleagues related to work matters) represents a "boundary-spanning demand" that blurs the boundaries separating work life from nonwork life (e.g., Clark, 2000; Voydanoff, 2005). This boundary-spanning demand is distinct from job-related demands such as long work hours and excessive pressures (Glavin & Schieman, 2012; Schieman & Glavin, 2008). Work contact, as a boundary-spanning demand, chips away at the border separating work life from other life domains. As such, it is considered a potential stressor. To alleviate this potential stress, the individual should request that their supervisor and other coworkers refrain from getting in touch with them outside of the workplace or after work hours (through any means of direct communication such as phone calls, text messaging, or email) to discuss work-related issues. In most cases, such requests are honored, and it makes it more enforceable when the individual makes such requests explicit, perhaps in writing. Organizations can even make a formal off-hour communication policy. Of course, during a time when more people work from home than ever before, work communication often occurs out of the physical office space. As such, a communicative rule such as "don't contact me while I am at home" is not realistic. The best one can do is segment by telling work colleagues "you can communicate with me by email or text anytime, but I'll respond during work hours and only during those hours."

To reiterate, communicative segmentation involves the management of others' expectations regarding boundaries (Kreiner, Hollensbe, & Sheep, 2009). That is, a boundary is erected by signaling to others that certain actions constitute boundary violations, hence the plea to respect one's boundaries. Consider the following survey item: "I have indicated to my boss that I cannot work past the end of my normal workday unless it is a rare circumstance." Here the individual has managed to erect a boundary around their family domain by communicating to their boss that the home is their sanctuary and to refrain from expecting them to engage in work-related matters during "family time" (such as evenings and weekends). By communicating their expectations to others (family members, coworkers, and bosses), the individual can segment the work and family domains assuming that these expectations are adhered to and violations do not occur. As such, communicative segmentation is likely to contribute to greater engagement in the protected domain, thus ensuring greater satisfaction in the same domain (Carlson, Ferguson, & Kacmar, 2016).

Going back to Kathy and the problems she has encountered at work and home: she decides to implement communicative segmentation too. She did this by telling her staff that they are free to contact her between the hours of 8:00 a.m. and 3:00 p.m., however not to call her after 4:00 p.m. (to hold those calls until the next morning).

9.2 Developing a Training Program Guided by the Principle of Segmentation

A training program can be developed that is guided by the segmentation principle and the suggested interventions of temporal, physical, behavior, and communicative segmentation (see Table 9.1). One plausible pedagogical method is the use of a well-established and validated measure[2] of

---

[2] A validated measure in psychometrics is usually an instrument that has been tested for the fact that the measured construct is real.

segmentation (Carlson, Ferguson, & Kacmar, 2016). See Table 9.2 for the survey items capturing these work-life balance interventions.

Specifically, the work-life balance instructor can educate employees on how to use *temporal segmentation* by showing specific survey items designed to capture this type of segmentation. Examples include "While at work, I try to manage blocks of time so that I can keep work separate from family." This item captures temporal segmentation in the work domain to ensure that family demands do not interfere with work, thereby protecting the work domain from other domains such as family life. "While at home, I try to manage my time such that family time is family time, not work time" is another survey item capturing temporal segmentation of the family domain. In this case, the instructor may encourage the workshop participants to respond to the survey items by stating their degree of agreement or disagreement with each item, which is then followed by a class discussion of how these items capture what participants do or don't do. This exercise should instruct participants on how to use segmentation to prevent negative spillover from work life to family life and vice versa.

A similar exercise can be implemented guided by the survey items capturing *physical, behavior, and communicative segmentation*. See the survey items in Table 9.2.

Table 9.2 *Survey measures of types of segmentation interventions*

- Keeping Family out of Work
  - Work-family: Temporal
    - While at work, I try to manage blocks of time so that I can keep work separate from family.
    - While at work, I try to manage my time such that work time is work time, not family time.
    - While at work, I manage my time to keep family demands out of work.
  - Work-family: Physical
    - When I'm physically at work, I try not to address family-related issues so I can focus on work.
    - When I'm in the workplace, I leave family matters at home so that I can focus on work.
    - When I walk in the door to work, I put away any family-related thoughts and turn my focus to work.
  - Work-family: Behavior
    - While at work, I use technology to help facilitate keeping work responsibilities separate from family responsibilities.

Table 9.2 (*cont.*)

- While at work, I use technology to help keep family demands out of my work life.
- While at work, I use technology to help limit dealing with family during work time.
- Work-family: Communicative
  - I communicate clearly to my family that I prefer not to be distracted by family demands while I'm at work.
  - I have indicated to my family that I cannot deal with family matters during work hours unless it is a rare circumstance.
  - I set expectations with my family to not contact me at work unless it's an emergency.
- Keeping Work out of Family
  - Family-work: Temporal
    - While at home, I try to manage blocks of time so that I can keep family separate from work.
    - While at home, I try to manage my time such that family time is family time, not work time.
    - While at home, I manage my time to keep work demands out of family time.
  - Family-work: Physical
    - When I'm physically at home, I try not to address work-related issues so I can focus on my family.
    - When I'm at home, I leave work matters at work so that I can focus on my family.
    - When I walk in the door at home, I put away any work-related thoughts and turn my focus to family.
  - Family-work: Behavioral
    - While at home, I use technology to help facilitate keeping family responsibilities separate from work responsibilities.
    - While at home, I use technology to help keep work demands out of my family life.
    - While at home, I use technology to help limit dealing with work during family time.
  - Family-work: Communicative
    - I communicate clearly to my coworkers/supervisors that I prefer not to be distracted by work demands while I'm at home.
    - I have indicated to my boss that I cannot work past the end of my normal workday unless it is a rare circumstance.
    - I set expectations with my coworkers/supervisors to not contact me at home unless it's an emergency.

Notes:
- Response scale is a 5-point Likert-type scale ranging from "Strongly Disagree" (1) to "Strongly Agree" (5).

Source: Carlson, Ferguson, and Kacmar (2016), p. 1158

9.3   Conclusion

We discussed the principle of segmentation and segmentation strategies balanced employees commonly use to prevent negative spillover from one domain to another. We described segmentation as a cognition-based approach to work-life balance that involves creating boundaries (or psychological walls) to insulate life domains. To reiterate, the goal is to prevent negative spillover from the segmented domain to other domains. We then discussed four different segmentation interventions: temporal, physical, behavior, and communicative. Temporal segmentation involves creating time boundaries. For example, employees segment work life from interference from family life (or vice versa) by making decisions and changes in their daily calendar. Physical segmentation involves physical boundaries. One can insulate a domain by making decisions to engage in domain-related activities within specified boundaries that are spatial in nature (e.g., the physical space of the home becomes the boundary protecting family life). Behavior segmentation involves behavior-based boundaries: an example may be the use of two email accounts to separate professional from personal life. Communicative segmentation involves managing boundaries with others: an example is to request supervisors and coworkers not to call at home to discuss job-related concerns during non-business hours.

We also discussed intervention programs that organizations can institutionalize to achieve higher levels of employee work-life balance based on these segmentation approaches. We suggested that the instructor use the well-established survey measure of segmentation to educate workshop participants on how to gauge the degree to which they engage in temporal, physical, behavior, and communicative segmentation to insulate negative affect experienced in work (family) life and prevent the spillover of bad feelings into family (work) life. Responding to the survey items should provide the workshop participants with insight into their own psychology of work-life balance. A class discussion could then ensue based on the self-assessment that can further consolidate learning.

It should be noted that most employees use segmentation when they experience negative affect at work to prevent this affect from spreading to family life (and conversely when they experience negative affect at home to prevent this affect from spreading to work life). As such, segmentation is about negative spillover. But what about positive spillover? That is, what do employees do when they experience positive affect in one domain? Do they erect boundaries or do they do the opposite, namely tear down those boundaries? Tearing down the psychological walls that segment life domains is what we call "integration," which is the topic of the next chapter.

References

Ashforth, B. E., Kreiner, G. E., & Fugate, M. (2000). All in a day's work: Boundaries and micro role transitions. *Academy of Management Review*, 25(3), 472–491.

Beutell, N. J. & Wittig-Berman, U. (1999). Predictors of work-family conflict and satisfaction with family, job, career, and life. *Psychological Reports*, 85(3), 893–903.

Bulger, C. A., Matthews, R. A., & Hoffman, M.E. (2007). Work and personal life boundary management: Boundary strength, work/personal life balance, and the segmentation-integration continuum. *Journal of Occupational Health Psychology*, 12(4), 365–375.

Carlson, D. S., Ferguson, M., & Kacmar, K. M. (2016). Boundary management tactics: An examination of the alignment with preferences in the work and family domains. *Journal of Behavioral and Applied Management*, 16(2), 1158–1174.

Chesley, N. (2005). Blurring boundaries? Linking technology use, spillover, individual distress, and family satisfaction. *Journal of Marriage and Family*, 67(5), 1237–1248.

Clark, S. C. (2000). Work/family border theory: A new theory of work/family balance. *Human Relations*, 53(6), 747–770.

Edwards, J. R. & Rothbard, N. P. (2000). Mechanisms linking work and family: Clarifying the relationship between work and family constructs. *Academy of Management Review*, 25(1), 178–199.

Glavin, P. & Schieman, S. (2012). Work-family role blurring and work-family conflict: The moderating influence of job resources and job demands. *Work & Occupations*, 39(1), 71–98.

Golden, A. G. & Geisler, C. (2007). Work-life boundary management and the personal digital assistant. *Human Relations*, 60(3), 519–551.

Kreiner, G. E., Hollensbe, E. C., & Sheep, B. L. (2009). Balancing borders and bridges: Negotiating the work-home interface via boundary work tactics. *Academy of Management Journal*, 52(4), 704–730.

Myrie, J. & Daly, K. (2009). The use of boundaries by self-employed, home based workers to manage work and family: A qualitative study in Canada. *Journal of Family Economic Issues*, 30(4), 386–398.

Park, Y., Fritz, C., & Jex, S. M. (2011). Relationships between work-home segmentation and psychological detachment from work: the role of communication technology use at home. *Journal of Occupational Health Psychology*, 16(4), 457–469.

Rau, B. L. & Hyland, M. A. M. (2002). Role conflict and flexible work arrangements: The effects on applicant attraction. *Personnel Psychology*, 55(1), 111–136.

Schieman, S. & Glavin, P. (2008). Trouble at the border? Gender, flexible work conditions, and the work-home interface. *Social Problems*, 55(4), 590–611.

Schieman, S. & Young, M. C. (2013). Are communications about work outside regular working hours associated with work-to-family conflict, psychological distress and sleep problems? *Work & Stress*, 27(3), 244–261.

Sirgy, M. J. (2002). *The psychology of quality of life*. Dordrecht, Netherlands: Kluwer Academic Publishers.

Sonnentag, S. (2012). Psychological detachment from work during leisure time the benefits of mentally disengaging from work. *Current Directions in Psychological Science*, 21(2), 114–118.

Sonnentag, S., Mojza, E. J., Binnewies, C., & Scholl, A. (2008). Being engaged at work and detached at home: A week-level study on work engagement, psychological detachment, and affect. *Work & Stress*, 22(3), 257–276.

Voydanoff, P. (2005). Consequences of boundary-spanning demands and resources for work-to-family conflict and perceived stress. *Journal of Occupational Health Psychology*, 10(4), 491–503.

Wegge, J., Schmidt, K., Parkes, C., & Van Dick, R. (2007). "Taking a sickie": Job satisfaction and job involvement as interactive predictors of absenteeism in a public organization. *Journal of Occupational & Organizational Psychology*, 80(1), 77–89.

CHAPTER 10

Integrating Roles and Domains

10.1 Integrating Roles and Domains

Integrating roles and life domains that house high levels of positive affect (or satisfaction) is an important personal intervention used by some people to help them achieve life balance. Doing so serves to maintain life satisfaction at acceptable levels. Family business owners who reside in the same building as their business (or in a nearby residence) are excellent examples of individuals who integrate roles and domains. Family members may help at the store – staffing the checkout stand, maintaining inventory, dealing with suppliers and customers, and so on. The store owner's work life is highly integrated with their nonwork life (family life, marital life, social life, material life, and perhaps community life too). The store is doing well in that it has a good stream of patrons, a good reputation in the neighborhood, and it generates a decent income that supports the family and a few other jobs in the community. Thus, the success of the store is a major source of satisfaction in work life, family life, marital life, social life, financial life, and community life. What is most interesting in this scenario is the notion of positive spillover, as there are no time and spatial boundaries between life domains. That is, satisfaction in one life domain spills over to other life domains, thus amplifying the combined satisfaction from the various domains on overall life satisfaction. Thus, the *positive spillover* serves to increase life satisfaction by integrating both work and nonwork domains.

Two related and highly similar theories dealing with the management of boundaries between life domains address the concepts of domain integration and positive spillover, namely *boundary theory* (Ashforth, Kreiner, & Fugate, 2000; Nippert-Eng, 1996) and *work-family border theory* (Clark, 2000). Boundary theory focuses on work and *nonwork* domains, whereas work-family border theory focuses more particularly on work and *family* domains. These theories make the case that people create psychological boundaries between work and nonwork domains. Some create boundaries to segment domains, while others create more permeable boundaries to allow the integration of roles. Our focus here is on integration. Specifically, the strength of boundaries refers to the level of flexibility and permeability of domain boundaries. Flexibility refers to the extent to which a mental boundary contracts or expands in time and space depending on the demands felt in that domain or another. For example, an individual may erect a work domain boundary with high flexibility (in terms of space and time) to allow them to work outside of both traditional workspaces and work times. In contrast, permeability refers to the degree to which affect experienced in one domain can spill over to another domain. For example, an individual who operates a family store would likely have high permeability between work and family as his employees are also his children.

Segmentation is viewed as one polar extreme on a continuum with integration on the other extreme. In relation to segmentation (one polar extreme along the segmentation-integration dimension) boundaries between work and family domains are highly impermeable and least flexible. Conversely, the opposite is true in relation to integration (the other polar extreme of the segmentation-integration dimension). That is, in integration we see the same boundaries as highly permeable and most flexible. Integration allows the individual to easily transition between work and family domains. This is the key benefit of integration.

Let's delve deeper into the concept of positive spillover. Experiences in work *and* nonwork life may spill over. That is, affect may spill over from work life to nonwork life and vice versa. This is what industrial/organizational psychologists commonly refer to as "affect spillover" (e.g., Edwards & Rothbard, 2000; Grzywacz & Carlson, 2007). *Affect spillover* can be either positive or negative. Positive affect spillover refers to a positive mood that transfers from one life domain to another. Conversely, negative spillover refers to negative mood spilling over from one domain to another.[1]

Consider the following case involving two individuals, Mike and Tom. Both men experience "+1" units of satisfaction in work life and "+3" units of satisfaction in family life. However, Tom decides to integrate work

---

[1] Affect spillover should be distinguished from *crossover effects*. Affect spillover refers to feelings caused by experiences in one life domain to influence another life domain. It is an intra-individual phenomenon (i.e., within an individual). In contrast, *crossover effect* is an inter-individual construct. It refers to emotional contagion between individuals whereby individuals are influenced by the emotions displayed by those around them (e.g., Demerouti, Bakker, & Schaufeli 2005; Hatfield, Cacioppo, & Rapson, 1994). Crossover effects are likely to be high when individuals are in physical proximity and close communications (Barsade, 2002; Neumann & Strack, 2000).

and family domains (e.g., by working at home and taking care of family responsibilities at work). Tom was highly successful in integrating work and family domains. Doing so increased his satisfaction in work life from "+1" to "+3," whereas his satisfaction in family life remained at "+3." Tom achieved work-life balance through positive spillover. In contrast, Mike did not bother to integrate the two domains; hence, he continued experiencing "+1" satisfaction in work life and "+3" in family life. In this case, positive spillover through domain integration resulted in greater satisfaction in family life for Tom, and as a result higher life satisfaction.

Thus, the principle of positive spillover states that positive affect in two life domains that are highly integrated amplify domain satisfaction, which in turn spills over to overall life satisfaction. That is, positive affect that spills over between life domains increases the level of satisfaction in both of those domains. For example, sharing positive work experiences increases family satisfaction because the act of sharing positive events facilitates a positive mood among family members and thus increases family satisfaction (e.g., Gable, Gonzaga, & Strachman, 2006; Heller & Watson, 2005). Furthermore, positive affect in one role can boost the level of motivation and energy to engage in another role in a neighboring domain. Thus, positive affect in one domain may increase the likelihood of successful performance in a different domain, resulting in increased satisfaction in that domain, which in turn increases life satisfaction overall (Edwards & Rothbard, 2000).

How can one improve integration and positive spillover from one life domain to another? There are four strategies to integrate life domains to achieve work-life balance: (1) temporal, (2) physical, (3) behavior, and (4) communicative. These integration strategies are the exact opposite of the segmentation interventions discussed in the previous chapter.

10.1.1   Temporal Integration

Participating in the gig economy is a good way to experience temporal integration. The gig economy refers to freelance and contract work, compared to work through permanent positions (Baldoma Jones, 2020; Warren, 2021). Examples of participating in the gig economy are working freelance for a ride-share service like Uber or Lyft or delivering food through an online delivery service like Grubhub, Doordash, or Uber Eats. Working in the gig economy provides a measure of work flexibility. Workers in industries that use computer software and the internet heavily are ideal for the gig economy. For example, journalists use their laptop computers and the internet to write stories and copyedit. They can do so from home and at times most convenient to them in ways that may not interfere with other responsibilities. As such, the concept of work-life balance has been recently reconceptualized to consider the emerging nature of the gig economy (Kelliher, Richardson, & Boiarintseva, 2019). The rise of gig work allows workers to integrate work life with other life domains, boosting productivity while enabling workers to achieve work-life balance (Malone, 2004; Gratton & Johns, 2013; Sundararajan, 2016).

Consider the following study that focused on Uber drivers in London (Berger et al., 2019). The study found that most of the drivers, although not earning much money, reported higher levels of life satisfaction than other non-gig workers. The researchers attributed the higher life satisfaction among the drivers to their preferences for flexibility and autonomy, which in turn helped them achieve work-life balance. The study highlighted the importance of non-monetary factors such as work-life balance in contributing to life satisfaction in the gig economy.

Yolanda is a good example of the use of integration to help achieve greater work-life balance. Yolanda is a nurse who has worked for over twenty years in the nursing industry. A few years ago, she decided to establish her own homecare service focusing on the elderly. She recruited ten young women who had their CAN (Certified Nursing Aide) license and hit the ground running. She also managed to establish a relationship with several rehabilitation facilities in the area, and she received referrals from them. She started out by providing home healthcare for three elderly patients, and the customer base recently grew to twenty-one patients. Yolanda is also married with two teenage children, all of whom are very helpful around the house. She manages her business from her home. She practices "temporal integration" by integrating the time at home with time spent running the homecare service business. Doing so allows her to manage both her household and business much more efficiently. She doesn't have the daily commute she had when she was working in several nursing homes located on the other side of town. She is certainly saving time working from home. Once in a while, she travels to her elderly patients' homes to check on things to ensure patient satisfaction with the service. In sum, her work life is highly integrated with her home life. Her business is growing and flourishing, further she feels that it is making a positive contribution to the community. She also feels good about her family. Her husband and children are helping out in both running the home healthcare business and the household. She experiences quite a bit of positive spillover because her work and nonwork domains are highly integrated contributing to a high level of life satisfaction.

Participating in the gig economy is a good way to integrate roles and domains – gig jobs (freelance and contract work) often allow workers to fuse work and nonwork domains through flexibility in terms of schedule and workplace.

10.1.2 Physical Integration

Teleworking is a good way to experience physical integration. People who telework have a greater opportunity to exercise psychological integration between and among life domains, compared to those who do not telework, through the physical environment (e.g., work from home). Researchers have increasingly studied teleworking in order to understand its impact on work-family conflict (e.g., Bailey & Kurland, 2002; Gajendran & Harrison, 2007; Kurland & Bailey, 1999; Mann & Holdsworth, 2003). Telework may take place during regular office hours as well as outside regular office hours ("after hours") and is considered an alternate work method. Telework should not be confused with "supplemental work" or "overtime."

Telework, as an integration strategy, tends to increase positive spill-over of domain satisfaction and decrease work-to-family conflict (the type of stress originating from work and spilling over into family life) due to increased flexibility and control over the pacing and scheduling of work as well as increased time at home (e.g., Duxbury, Higgins, & Mills, 1992; Duxbury, Higgins, & Thomas, 1996; Jostell & Hemlin, 2018). However, there may be situations in which integration is a source of work-to-family conflict – stress from work spilling over to family life. Telework brings down the border between work and family domains, and this could lead to interference with family affairs due to work demand, which may add to – not diminish – work-family conflict (Allen, Golden, & Shockley, 2015). Lack of a border between work life and home life may also make it difficult to mentally disengage from work (e.g., Boswell & Olson-Buchanan, 2007; Golden, 2012; Hill et al., 2010), thus contributing to work-family conflict. This is a major cause of an imbalanced life.

Going back to Yolanda, one can also see elements of physical integration. Both work and family life take place in the same location, namely at home. In other words, she manages her business from her home.

10.1.3 Behavior Integration

Integration occurs through behavior designed to combine work and non-work roles and domains. Behavioral integration refers to engaging in certain behaviors (e.g., use of the same resources) for the roles across different life domains. A good example of behavior integration involves how people build their relationships across roles and domains to achieve success in life. There is a particular theory supported by substantial empirical evidence suggesting that relational coordination is key to organizational success (Follett, 1949). The theory posits that relationships built around shared goals, knowledge, and coordination among multiple stakeholders across work boundaries are key to organizational effectiveness. Much evidence has accumulated in the management literature supporting this theory. See Bolton, Logan, and Gittell (2021) for a systematic review of this literature.

The same can be said about achieving individual success in life. That is, people become happier in life when they become successful in leveraging personal relationships to meet work demand. Conversely, business relationships are leveraged to meet personal demands (e.g., nonwork demands in family roles).

Let's go back to the case of Yolanda. To be successful in her home healthcare service, Yolanda had to tap into her personal network of friends and associates to spread the word and gain referrals. When questioned about her success running the business so far, she claimed that her personal connections have been key. This is a good example of how people engage in certain behaviors, in this case using personal connections for business purposes, to achieve integration and success in life at large.

10.1.4 *Communicative Integration*

The use of information and communication technologies (ICTs) such as the internet and smartphones have blurred the boundaries between work and nonwork (Colbert, Yee, & George, 2016; Derks, 2016; Derks et al., 2016; Jackson, Young, & Sander, 2020; Piszczek, 2017). Communicative integration refers to the use of the same ICTs across life domains. ICTs allow people to move from one role to another, one life domain to another, more frequently and effortlessly – especially when they use an integration strategy of work-life balance. For example, while working, a person can achieve more integration by easily replying to friends and family instantly using their smartphones. That is, workers can answer personal messages with little-to-no negative impact on their job performance. Integration of professional and personal lives is increasingly commonplace for many organizations and workers. As such, the use of ICTs can assist in integrating work life with nonwork life.

Consider the following study conducted by Wang, Gao, and Lin (2019). This study examined the role of ICTs in family-to-work conflict and work-family balance satisfaction, and the moderating effect of integration in that process. The study findings indicated that high levels of ICT use led to higher levels of family-to-work interference. That is, the use of ICTs can help those who use an integration strategy to maintain work-life balance, but conversely, the use of ICTs negatively affects those who use a segmentation strategy to keep their work life separate from personal life.

Going back to Yolanda, the owner of a home healthcare service. Yolanda uses ICTs to run both her business and household. She efficiently communicates with her nurse aides mostly by phone and sometimes by text. The use of phone and text is conducive to effective integration and positive spillover.

10.2 Developing a Training Program Guided by the Integration Principle

As discussed above, integration usually occurs in situations involving temporal, physical, behavior, and communicative integration. These interventions facilitate integration and positive spillover, and in doing so they help achieve work-life balance and increase life satisfaction (see Table 10.1).

With respect to *temporal integration*, the instructor can address how the *gig economy* plays an important role in integrating work life with nonwork life through providing flexibility in terms of work schedule. However, before discussing how workers can be educated to use gig work to achieve work-life balance through integration and positive spillover, the instructor has to be aware of the caveats. Warren (2021) argued that gig workers lack a safety net that is common in formal employment. They experience unpredictability in both work-time and income, work intensification, and financial hardship that all impact work-life balance. This industrial relations scholar recommended that national policies should be formulated to protect gig workers and enhance work-life imbalance arising from the disadvantages mentioned above. She also recommended that gig workers of specific organizations (e.g., Uber) should consider unionizing. In doing so, they may be in a stronger position to demand better conditions. As such, firms could be encouraged to work only with unionized gig workers. Work-life balance instructors should highlight these caveats when discussing the gig economy.

Going back to how gig workers can take better advantage of their gig work to integrate their life domains and experience positive spillover, here are some suggestions:

Table 10.1 *Integrating roles and life domains*

Intervention	Description	References
Temporal integration	Integrate work and nonwork domains by integrating work and nonwork schedules (e.g., gig work).	Kelliher, Richardson, and Boiarintseva (2019)
Physical integration	Integrate work and nonwork domains by working and living in the same physical space (e.g., telework).	Gajendran and Harrison (2007)
Behavior integration	Integrating work and nonwork domains by using personal resources for work purposes and vice versa (e.g., use of personal connections for work purposes).	Bolton, Logan, and Gittell (2021)
Communicative integration	Integrating work and nonwork domains by using the same information communication technologies to attend to both work and nonwork matters (e.g., using the same email for work and personal matters).	Wang, Gao, and Lin (2019)

- Gig workers can enhance the way they integrate their life domains by using their freedom to structure both their work and nonwork time. As such, time management is important. This is due to the fact that gig workers have to deal with multiple stakeholders and different products. They have to self-impose a time structure when there is no structure in place.
- Gig workers have the opportunity to be involved in a variety of projects that allow them to learn new skills. They apply the new learning across their varied social roles creating greater positive spillover, which in turn contributes to life satisfaction.
- They can take breaks when they need to and exercise more because they have more control over their time. These positive health effects provide benefits across life domains.

With respect to *physical integration*, the instructor of the work-life balance workshop can educate employees about the types of telework available and how telework allows integration of work and nonwork roles and domains by sharing the same physical space (i.e., working from home). There are two types of telework: routine telework and situational telework. Routine telework involves working remotely on an ongoing and regular basis. In contrast, situational telework is granted by management on a case-by-case basis. That is, it is situation specific. Employees should inquire about their organization's policy regarding telework, and whether telework is usually encouraged and granted routinely or situationally. If the organization encourages and grants telework opportunities to its employees routinely, then Human Resources is very likely to have a concrete policy about telework and the organization's rules and regulations concerning telework. On the other hand, if the organization does not grant telework routinely (and as such does not have a set of well-articulated policies) then it would be advisable to encourage employees to take the initiative to do the following:

- develop a statement of purpose to identify the intended benefits or outcomes of teleworking;
- spell out the exact nature of the telework to be performed, including where and when it will be performed;
- identify needs and support equipment necessary for the telework (e.g., laptops, printer, phone, supplies, internet service, IT support);
- address possible cybersecurity issues (if and when they apply);
- identify aspects of the work that are likely to be modified in telework;
- address any anticipated problems and solutions regarding how the telework may affect coworkers and work supervision;
- describe how a record-keeping system can be developed and maintained to help management monitor the telework;
- describe the reporting of the actual telework and outcomes to management;
- describe how the telework can be evaluated by management and whether the compensation plan should or should not be adjusted accordingly;
- describe how management can communicate with the teleworker routinely through specified telecommunication means (e.g., telephone, email, teleconference, home visits) and the desired frequency of this type of communication; and
- address unexpected contingencies that could impact the telework arrangement (e.g., personal illness, sickness of a family member, pandemic and other natural and man-made disasters).

With respect to *behavior integration*, the use of personal resources for work purposes (and vice versa) helps employees integrate work and nonwork roles and domains. The instructor could focus on social capital to illustrate the use of behavior integration. As such, employees could be encouraged to consider the scenario involving Yolanda. As a reminder, Yolanda is a nurse who recently started her own homecare service caring for the elderly.

She has a staff of ten nursing aides and has established relationships with several rehabilitation facilities in her area from which she frequently receives referrals. In the beginning, she started by providing home health-care to three patients, but her customer base has grown to twenty-one patients. Yolanda is also married with two teenage children, all of whom help with both the house and the business.

In the context of this scenario, the workshop participants are encouraged to contemplate how Yolanda promotes her home healthcare service. Can she use her personal connections to promote her business? If so, how? This scenario could generate a class discussion in which participants would be encouraged to use examples from their own lives in which they used social capital built in the context of one role to enhance performance in another role. Participants are then encouraged to discuss how doing so helped them integrate their work and nonwork domains, which in turn helped achieve greater work-life balance and life satisfaction.

With respect to the *communicative integration*, below are integration suggestions for the work-life balance instructor that can be incorporated into a training seminar or workshop. These are the exact opposite of the segmentation recommendations we discussed in the previous chapter.

Suggestions for supervisors:

- Supervisors should communicate their expectations regarding the use of information communication technologies (ICTs) at home for work purposes. That is, they should develop and communicate to their subordinates "an acceptable use" policy that promotes integration and positive spillover. Employees should be encouraged to use ICTs and respond in due time to all work-related messages at all times (nonworking hours and weekends too).
- Supervisors should act as "role models" for new employees. Specifically, they should demonstrate behaviors that promote integration and positive spillover. Doing so is likely to communicate the benefits of using ICTs to help integrate work life with nonwork domains.

Suggestions for employees:

- Employees are encouraged to use the same ICTs to attend to both personal and professional matters. They can use the same email account to process personal and work-related communications, the same computer or laptop to complete work-related and nonwork-related projects, and the same phone to communicate with people at work as well as family and friends.

- Employees could inform their supervisor and coworkers to feel free to communicate with them 24/7, and that their supervisor and coworkers should not hesitate to communicate using any type of ICT at any time.

10.3 Conclusion

In the previous chapter we discussed segmentation as a personal intervention to help achieve greater work-life balance and life satisfaction. Segmentation works best when people experience negative feelings in one life domain that can spill over and "infect" other domains. The result can diminish overall life satisfaction. Hence, segmentation is a personal intervention that serves to protect life satisfaction from dipping due to negative spillover. The opposite occurs with integration. Integration is commonly used to take advantage of positive feelings in one or more domains that can spill over to other life domains. There are many situations and occupations that benefit from an integration rather than a segmentation type of work-life balance intervention. Entrepreneurs and owners/managers of small businesses are a case in point. To be successful in their professional roles, they have to adapt by integrating their work and nonwork domains. They cannot afford to do otherwise, assuming organizational success is a major life goal. In contrast, segmentation is best for other professionals employed in major companies with high work demand and a family that demands substantial time, energy, and other resources. This is because high demand in work and nonwork roles are likely to lead to role conflict, which in turn causes stress and strain, detracting from life satisfaction.

In this chapter we concentrated on integration as a personal intervention serving to balance work life with other important life domains such as family life, social life, and leisure life. We made the case that integration is best for work-life balance when life domains are highly interdependent. Integration takes advantage of positive spillover to increase life satisfaction. Positive spillover refers to the mental process by which the individual allows positive feelings invested in one life domain to spill over to other domains. We discuss four ways that people use to integrate their life domains to achieve work-life balance: temporal integration, physical integration, behavior integration, and communicative integration.

We discussed how gig projects such as freelance and contract work can provide workers a great deal of schedule flexibility. The rise of gig work allows workers to attend to work matters at times traditionally allocated for nonwork matters and vice versa. This is an example of temporal integration – integrating work life with other life domains using scheduling flexibility.

Integration can also be achieved by manipulating the physical space (e.g., using one's place of residence to attend to job-related matters as well as personal matters). This is the essence of telework. As such, telework should be viewed as an integration strategy that decreases work-to-family conflict (the type of stress originating from work and spilling over into family life) due to increased flexibility and control over where and when the employee performs their job.

We also discussed how integration can be achieved through actual behavior such as the use of personal connections across domains. We focused on how employees use personal connections for work purposes; and conversely how work connections are used for personal purposes. Such cross-domain use of personal resources is a key characteristic of the integration of work and nonwork roles and domains.

Communicative integration involves the use of ICTs (e.g., the internet and smartphones) to move from one role to another, one life domain to another, more frequently and effortlessly. In other words, the use of ICTs plays an important role in integrating work life with nonwork life.

We also discussed intervention programs that organizations can institutionalize to achieve higher levels of employee work-life balance based on these personal strategies. We discussed how organizations can develop a training program around the integration principle and encourage selected employees (only those who are likely to benefit the most, such as managers) to integrate their lives by manipulating temporal, physical, behavior, and communicative elements.

References

Allen, T. D., Golden, T. D., & Shockley, K. M. (2015). How effective is telecommuting? Assessing the status of our scientific findings. *Psychological Science in the Public Interest*, 16(2), 40–68.

Ashforth, B. E., Kreiner, G. E., & Fugate, M. (2000). All in a day's work: Boundaries and micro role transitions. *Academy of Management Review*, 25(3), 472–491.

Baldoma Jones, P. (2020). 7 reasons why the gig economy is here to stay. *Celerative*, March 8, 2020. (www.celerative.com/blog/7-reasons-why-the-gig-economy-is-here-to-stay).

Barsade, S. G. (2002). The ripple effect: Emotional contagion and its influence on group behavior. *Administrative Science Quarterly*, 47(4), 644–675.

Bailey, D. E. & Kurland, N. B. (2002). A review of telework research: Findings, new directions, and lessons for the study of modern work. *Journal of Organizational Behavior*, 23(4), 383–400.

Berger, T., Frey, C. B., Levin, G., & Danda, S. R. (2019). Uber happy? Work and well-being in the "gig economy". *Economic Policy*, 34(99), 429–477.

Bolton, R., Logan, C., & Gittell, J. H. (2021). Revisiting relational coordination: A systematic review. *Journal of Applied Behavioral Science*, 57(3), 290–322.

Boswell, W. R. & Olson-Buchanan, J. B. (2007). The use of communication technologies after hours: The role of work attitudes and work-life conflict. *Journal of Management*, 33(4), 592–610.

Clark, S. C. (2000). Work/family border theory: A new theory of work/family balance. *Human Relations*, 53(6), 747–770.

Colbert, A., Yee, N. & George, G. (2016). The digital workforce and the workplace of the future. *Academy of Management Journal*, 59(3), 731–739.

Demerouti, E., Bakker, A. B., & Schaufeli, W. B. (2005). Spillover and crossover of exhaustion and life satisfaction among dual-earner parents. *Journal of Vocational Behavior*, 67 (2), 266–289.

Derks, D., Bakker, A. B., Peters, P., & van Wingerden, P. (2016). Work-related smartphone use, work-family conflict and family role performance: The role of segmentation preference. *Human Relations*, 69(5), 1045–1068.

Duxbury, L. E., Higgins, C. A., & Mills, S. (1992). After-hours telecommuting and work-family conflict: A comparative analysis. *Information Systems Research*, 3(2), 173–190.

Duxbury, L. E., Higgins, C. A., & Thomas, D. R. (1996). Work and family environments and the adoption of computer-supported supplemental work-at-home. *Journal of Vocational Behavior*, 49(1), 1–23.

Edwards, J. R. & Rothbard, N. P. (2000). Mechanisms linking work and family: Clarifying the relationship between work and family constructs. *Academy of Management Review*, 25(1), 178–199.

Follett, M. P. (1949). Coordination. In L. Urwick (Ed.), *Freedom and coordination: Lectures in business organization by Mary Parker Follett* (pp. 61–76). London: Routledge.

Gable, S. L., Gonzaga, G. C., & Strachman, A. (2006). Will you be there for me when things go right? Supportive responses to positive event disclosures. *Journal of Personality and Social Psychology*, 91(5), 904–917.

Gajendran, R. S. & Harrison, D. A. (2007). The good, the bad, and the unknown about telecommuting: Meta-analysis of psychological mediators and individual consequences. *Journal of Applied Psychology*, 92(6), 1524–1541.

Golden, T. D. (2012). Altering the effects of work and family conflict on exhaustion: Telework during traditional and nontraditional work hours. *Journal of Business and Psychology*, 27(3), 255–269.

Gratton, L. & Johns, T. (2013). The third wave of virtual work. *Harvard Business Review*, Jan–Feb, 2–9.

Grzywacz, J. G. & Carlson, D. S. (2007). Conceptualizing work-family balance: Implications for practice and research. *Advances in Developing Human Resources*, 9(4), 455–471.

Hatfield, E., Cacioppo, J. T., & Rapson, R. L. (1994). *Emotional contagion*. Cambridge: Cambridge University Press.

Heller, D. & Watson, D. (2005). The dynamic spillover of satisfaction between work and marriage: The role of time, mood and personality. *Journal of Applied Psychology*, 90(6), 1273–1279.

Hill, E. J., Erickson, J. J., Holmes, E. K., & Ferris, M. (2010). Workplace flexibility, work hours, and work-life conflict: Finding an extra day or two. *Journal of Family Psychology*, 24(3), 349–358.

Jackson, D., Young, V., & Sander, A. (2020). Information and communication technologies and work-life balance: Practical recommendations for employers and individuals. In M. Peaslee Levine (Ed.), *Interpersonal Relationships* (pp. 137–144). London: IntechOpen.

Jostell, D. & Hemlin, S. (2018). After hours teleworking and boundary management: Effects on work-family conflict. *Work*, 60(3), 475–483.

Kelliher, C., Richardson, J., & Boiarintseva, G. (2019). All of work? All of life? Reconceptualising work-life balance for the 21st century. *Human Resource Management Journal*, 29(2), 97–112.

Kurland, N. B. & Bailey, D. E. (1999). The advantages and challenges of working here, there anywhere, and anytime. *Organizational Dynamics*, 28(2), 53–68.

Malone, T. W. (2004). *The future of work: how the new order of business will shape your organization, your management style, and your life*. Boston, MA: Harvard Business School Press.

Mann, S. & Holdsworth, L. (2003). The psychological impact of teleworking: Stress, emotions and health. *New Technology, Work and Employment*, 18(3), 196–211.

Neumann, R. & Strack, F. (2000). "Mood contagion": the automatic transfer of mood between persons. *Journal of Personality and Social Psychology*, 79(2), 211–224.

Nippert-Eng, C. E. (1996). *Home and work*. Chicago: The University of Chicago Press.

Piszczek, M. M. (2017). Boundary control and controlled boundaries: organizational expectations for technology use at the work-family interface. *Journal of Organizational Behavior*, 38(4), 592–611.

Sundararajan, A. (2016). *The sharing economy: The end of employment and the rise of crowd-based capitalism*. Cambridge, MA: MIT Press.

Wang, X., Gao, L., & Lin, Z (2019). Help or harm? The effects of ICTs usage on work-life balance. *Journal of Managerial Psychology*, 34(8), 533–545.

Warren, T. (2021). Work-life balance and gig work: "Where are we now" and "where to next" with the work-life balance agenda? *Journal of Industrial Relations*, 63(4), 522–545.

Engaging in Value-Based Compensation

11.1 Engaging in Value-Based Compensation

Individuals try to maintain an acceptable level of life satisfaction by increasing the salience of satisfying life domains while decreasing the salience of dissatisfying life domains (e.g., Edwards & Rothbard, 2000; Greenhaus, Collins, & Shaw, 2003; Lee & Sirgy, 2018; Sirgy, 2002; Sirgy & Lee, 2016). This is referred to as *value-based compensation*. It is a cognition-based strategy in which the individual reacts to decreases in satisfaction in a given role by decreasing the perceived importance of that role. Value-based compensation is akin to behavior-based compensation (see Chapter 6). Recall our discussion on behavior-based compensation. We described this phenomenon as withdrawing from a dissatisfying role and engaging in an alternative, more satisfying role. "Withdrawing" and "engaging" are forms of behavior designed to compensate. In contrast, value-based compensation involves changing the salience or perceived importance of specific roles – compensation occurs through a cognitive change in valuation instead of a change in behavior.

To reiterate, value-based compensation refers to a cognition-based strategy in which the individual reacts to decreases in satisfaction in a given role by decreasing the perceived importance of that role (and ultimately the corresponding life domain). Conversely, increases in satisfaction in a given role lead to increases in the perceived importance of that role (and ultimately the corresponding life domain). Thus, individuals try to achieve balance in life and maintain life satisfaction by increasing the salience of the satisfying life domains while decreasing the salience of dissatisfying life domains.

Consider the following example. Jonathon is a freelance programmer. He has done very well doing freelance programming work for several companies. Recently, he has encountered problems with two of his major clients. The people he had previously been working with at these companies retired and were replaced by others who have different agendas and their own contacts with other freelancers. As such, he lost these major accounts. He then discovered that his wife has been cheating on him, which was extremely upsetting. He is now preparing for divorce. As such, he is feeling very unhappy in both work and marital life. His satisfaction with life over-all has plummeted as a result. Jonathon is a devout Catholic and attends mass weekly. He joined a support group at his church – this group meets once a week in the evening to discuss and share their problems and ulti-mately pray together as a way to help cope. Jonathon is now feeling trans-formed. Religion is now playing a major role in his life. He has turned to Jesus Christ and the Catholic Church for support and comfort. His religious life is now very important to him. It takes precedence over his work, his marriage and love life, his leisure life, his social life, and all other life domains. Increasing the value of his religious life helps improve his declining life satisfaction because of his problems with work and marriage. By elevating the importance of his religious life above and beyond these other life domains, he is feeling a significant increase in satisfaction in his religious life, which in turn is compensating for the satisfaction decline in both work and marital life. Thus, increasing the psychological value placed on religion helped him amplify the satisfaction he feels in his religious life; and this is in essence what value-based compensation is.

How do people implement value-based compensation to help achieve work-life balance and maintain a semblance of overall life satisfaction? Employees can effectively implement value-based compensation by (1) sequencing work and nonwork goals and (2) revising existing work and family goals and selecting new goals (Hirschi, Shockley, & Zacher, 2019). Let's discuss these personal interventions in more detail.

11.1.1   Sequencing Work and Nonwork Goals

One way to increase the salience of satisfying domains while decreasing the salience of dissatisfying domains is to sequence work and nonwork goals (e.g., Hirschi, Shockley, & Zacher, 2019; Johnson, Chang, & Lord, 2006; Wrosch et al., 2003). Sequencing is a form of goal restructuring. This personal intervention involves reprioritizing goals sequentially so that short-term priority is given to more attainable goals. Specifically, work and nonwork goals are either prioritized in the short term or the long term, depending on goal priority coupled with goal progress.

Consider the case of Tamara, a 35-year-old assistant professor of neu-roscience at a research university. She is forging a research program on the effects of cannabis on learning and cognitive functioning in humans.

This is her third year at the university. So far, she has conducted several studies, and the study findings were published in three well-established academic journals in psychology. However, to achieve tenure and promotion at her university she has to invest more time and energy in her research to produce yet another three to four journal publications to ensure that her record will be evaluated positively during her fifth year. Tamara started dating when she first arrived at the university and forged a romantic relationship with a biology professor at the same university. His name is Seth, a recent divorcee, and an associate professor with tenure. The relationship blossomed and they were married after a few months of dating. For the last year or so, Tamara and Seth have been discussing having children. However, they decided to postpone having children until she makes tenure and is promoted in a couple of years. However, Tamara has been apprehensive about her biological clock and the risk of genetic defects because of her age. Consequently, they decided to take drastic action by freezing her eggs to allow her ample time to concentrate on her career before getting pregnant and starting a family. Postponing pregnancy until she gains tenure and promotion is a good example of "sequencing work and nonwork goals." In this case, Tamara has decided to concentrate on her work goals (shorter-term) followed by starting a family (longer-term). As such, she has placed less importance on the goal of getting pregnant (decreasing the salience of family life, temporarily) while placing more importance on achieving tenure and promotion (increasing the salience of work life, temporarily).

To reiterate, if work and nonwork goals cannot be jointly achieved, people try to temporarily place less salience on a certain goal, planning to pursue this goal at a later point in time. That is, sometimes, and for some people, achieving work-life balance necessitates tradeoffs of goals in work and nonwork domains – because work and nonwork goals often cannot be achieved simultaneously. This personal intervention allows individuals to use their resources one goal at a time to avoid resource drain. In other words, people prioritize a work or nonwork goal that promotes subsequent goal attainment in another life domain. Of course, the challenge with this work-life balance intervention is that the temporarily unattainable goal is set aside while the more achievable goal is pursued.

11.1.2 Revising Existing Work and Nonwork Goals and Selecting New Goals

Increasing the salience of satisfying domains while decreasing the salience of dissatisfying ones can also be achieved by abandoning work and nonwork goals that the individual realizes are unachievable (e.g., Brandstätter, Herrmann, & Schüler, 2013; Hirschi, Shockley, & Zacher, 2019; Johnson, Chang, & Lord, 2006; Wrosch et al., 2003). Revising or abandoning unattainable goals prevents one from fruitlessly pursuing goals likely to generate negative feelings as a result of failure. As such, work-life balance can be achieved by revising existing goals and selecting new goals in work and nonwork domains. Such intervention ensures that the revised goals (or new goals) can generate success in both domains contributing to domain satisfaction and life satisfaction overall. The net result is also some sense of balance. Revising existing work and nonwork goals also means changing expectations for goal attainment – the desired level of a goal is lowered or the goal is completely abandoned.

Going back to Tamara's case, let's move forward in time. She is in her third year and was just evaluated by the Personnel Committee in her department. The evaluation was not good. The Personnel Committee stated that she has not made sufficient progress toward tenure and promotion, and she is very likely to be denied both given her current research and publications trajectory. She was confronted with a harsh reality: achieving her life goal of tenure and promotion at a prestigious research university is unattainable for her. As a result, she had to revise her career goals by lowering her expectations and perhaps settling for a faculty position at a more teaching-oriented university. Although she considered this possible move as a demotion, the new goal was nevertheless more realistic given the recent evaluation from the Personnel Committee and the painful disappointment of not making sufficient progress toward tenure and promotion. She believed that she would be a happier person at a more teaching-oriented college – that she can achieve her career goals plus raise a family (i.e., achieve work-life balance). She applied to a nearby teaching college for a faculty position in the Psychology Department and was accepted. And yes indeed, she managed to obtain tenure and promotion after her first year at the new college. She is now 39 years old. Thank goodness she and her husband decided to freeze her eggs. She is raising a family now and has a balanced life. She is a happier person.

11.2   Developing a Training Program Guided by the Principle of Value-Based Compensation

As suggested above, value-based compensation involves (1) sequencing work and nonwork goals and (2) revising existing work and nonwork goals and selecting new goals. Doing so facilitates work-life balance, which in turn serves to contribute to life satisfaction (see Table 11.1).

Table 11.1 *Engaging in value-based compensation*

Intervention	Description	References
Sequencing work and nonwork goals	Prioritize life goals and sequence them – determine which should be pursued in the short term and which in the long term.	Hirschi, Shockley, and Zacher (2019)
Revising existing work and nonwork goals and selecting new goals	Revise goals – goals that are difficult to achieve should be either abandoned or modified. New goals that are realistically achievable should replace those that are difficult to achieve.	Hirschi, Shockley, and Zacher (2019)

A training session can be developed around these two value-based compensation principles. With respect to the first principle (*sequencing work and nonwork goals*), the instructor can ask participants to generate a list of their life goals in terms of life domains such as work life, family life, marital or love life, health and safety, financial life, social and leisure life, among others (see Table 11.2). The instructor could then illustrate using Tamara's story – the aspiring professor whose life goals include achieving tenure/promotion and starting a family at the same time (near future). Tamara is currently pursuing a total of three life goals, as reflected in the "Life Goals" column of Table 11.2: A ("I want to achieve tenure and promotion"), B ("I want to start a family"), and C ("I want to be healthy and fit"). A and B are rated as "10" in the "Goal Priorities" column, indicating that they are the most important. As such, the attention of the workshop participants should be directed to these two most important goals. The second column in the table shows the intended time frame for pursuing each goal. As shown in the table, both goals are being pursued in the present or short term ("PST"). Make sure that the participants understand that these two most important goals cannot be achieved at the same time – they conflict. Pursuing one goal is likely to detract from achieving the other. Once the participants recognize the nature of the goal conflict, the instructor then describes how Tamara reconciles the goal conflict by revising the sequencing of her goal pursuit. A tradeoff decision is made. Specifically, Goal B (starting a family) had to be put on hold until Goal A (achieving tenure and promotion) is met. This is indicated in Table 11.2 by "DFLT"

Table 11.2 *How did Tamara go about revising the sequencing of her life goals*

Life Goals	Goal Priorities	Current Sequencing of Goal Pursuit {Present/Short-Term (PST) vs. Distant Future/Long-Term (DFLT)}	Revised Sequencing of Goal Pursuit {Present/Short-Term (PST) vs. Distant Future/Long-Term (DFLT)}
A: I want to achieve tenure and promotion	10	PST	PST
B: I want to start a family	10	PST	DFLT
C: I want to be healthy and fit	8	PST	PST
D: I want my house to be well-maintained and beautiful	7	DFLT	DFLT
E: I want to travel and see the world	5	DFLT	DFLT
F: I want to spend more time with my close friends	6	DFLT	DFLT

Notes:
- **Goal Priorities** = 10-point rating scale: "1 = Least Important"; "10 = Most Important"
- **Current Sequencing of Goal Pursuit** = 2-point scale: "PST =Present or Short-Term" versus "DFLT = Distant Future or Long-Term"
- **Revised Sequencing of Goal Pursuit** = 2-point scale: "PST =Present or Short-Term" versus "DFLT = Distant Future or Long-Term"

in the third column ("Revised Sequencing of Goal Pursuit"), which means that Tamara has revised the sequencing of her goal pursuit by postponing the pursuit of Goal B (starting a family) to the distant future. This goal is now relegated to long-term pursuit, not short-term.

After working through the Tamara illustration, the instructor could then provide the participants with a template that looks like Table 11.3. Participants are then asked to complete the table based on their own life goals. That is, they should list their life goals, rate their priority, indicate the current sequencing of goal pursuit, followed by an assessment of conflict between or among the most important life goals, and make tradeoff decisions regarding which goal should be pursued short term and which long term.

With respect to the second principle (*revising existing work and nonwork goals and selecting new goals*), the instructor can illustrate how Tamara

Table 11.3 *Revising sequencing of the pursuit of important life goals*

Life Goals	Goal Priorities	Current Sequencing of Goal Pursuit {Present/ Short-Term (PST) vs. Distant Future/Long-Term (DFLT)}	Revised Sequencing of Goal Pursuit {Present/Short-Term (PST) vs. Distant Future/ Long-Term (DFLT)}
A:			
B:			
C:			
D:			
E:			
F:			

Notes:
- **Goal Priority** = 10-point rating scale: "1 = Least Important"; "10 = Most Important"
- **Current Sequencing of Goal Pursuit** = 2-point scale: "PST =Present or Short-Term" versus "DFLT = Distant Future or Long-Term"
- **Revised Sequencing of Goal Pursuit** = 2-point scale: "PST =Present or Short-Term" versus "DFLT = Distant Future or Long-Term"

revised her life goals given her failure to make sufficient progress toward tenure and promotion at her university. Tamara's situation could be illustrated by walking the workshop participants through Table 11.4. Note the table has four columns; two columns to record initial priorities and progress ("Time 1") and two columns to record changes in priority and progress after goal revision ("Time 2"). Time 1 captures the time interval when the Personnel Committee evaluated Tamara's scholarly progress toward tenure and promotion, and Time 2 captures the time interval after the Personnel Committee's evaluation. In the context of each time interval, we see a column for "Goal Priorities" and another for "Progress toward Goal Attainment." Tamara's two most important life goals (A: "I want to achieve tenure and promotion at my current university"; and B: "I want to start a family") are both scored as "10" in Time 1, signaling that they are extremely important life goals. However, lack of progress toward attaining these life goals is indicated in the second column (Time 1): "2" and "1" respectively. Given the lack of progress toward tenure and promotion, Tamara revised her career goal related to her desire to achieve tenure and promotion at her current university (Goal A). The priority rating of this life goal went from "10 = Most Important" to "1 = Least Important." Because she has abandoned this goal, she has managed to replace this goal with "I want to achieve tenure and promotion at a teaching-oriented

Table 11.4 *How did Tamara go about changing her life goals as a function of her actual circumstances*

Life Goals	Goal Priorities (Time 1)	Progress toward Goal Attainment (Time 1)	Goal Priorities (Time 2)	Progress toward Goal Attainment (Time 2)
A: I want to achieve tenure and promotion at my current university	10	2	1	1
B: I want to start a family	10	1	10	7
C: I want to be healthy and fit	8	6	8	7
D: I want my house to be well-maintained and beautiful	7	5	8	7
E: I want to travel and see the world	5	1	5	1
F: I want to spend more time with my close friends	6	5	6	5
G: I want to achieve tenure and promotion at a teaching-oriented college nearby	2	1	10	8

Notes:
- **Goal Priorities** = 10-point rating scale: "1 = Least Important"; "10 = Most Important"
- **Progress toward Goal Attainment** = 10-point rating scale: "1 = No Progress at all" to "10 = Very Close to Goal Attainment"

college nearby" (Goal G) while still holding on to her other most important life goal: "I want to start a family" (Goal B). The table also captures the fact that she made significant progress toward achieving her new career goal (Goal G at Time 2) and wanting to start a family (Goal B at Time 2).

After discussing this example, the instructor could then provide the participants with a template (see Table 11.5). Participants are then asked to complete the table based on their own life goals and how they could revise their life goals as a direct function of progress toward goal attainment (or actual goal attainment). Doing so should help assess the viability of their life goals and make decisions about possibly revising these goals as a function of one's actual circumstances.

Table 11.5 *Assessing one's life goals, progress toward goal attainment,*
and making decisions about revising these goals

Life Goals	Goal Priorities (Time 1)	Progress toward Goal Attainment (Time 1)	Goal Priorities (Time 2)	Progress toward Goal Attainment (Time 2)
A:				
B:				
C:				
D:				
E:				
F:				
G:				

Notes:
- **Goal Priorities** = 10-point rating scale: "1 = Least Important"; "10 = Most Important"
- **Progress toward Goal Attainment** = 10-point rating scale: "1 = No Progress at all" to "10 = Very Close to Goal Attainment"

11.3 Conclusion

In this chapter we discussed the concept of value-based compensation. We defined this concept as changing the perceived importance of work and nonwork roles and life domains based on the level of satisfaction associated with these roles and domains. Specifically, individuals place greater value on those roles/domains they find satisfying and less value on those role/domains they find dissatisfying. Making changes in the way they perceive the importance of roles/domains serves to maintain an acceptable level of life satisfaction. In other words, people "compensate" for the dissatisfaction they experience in roles/domains by deflating the negative feelings in relation to the dissatisfying roles/domains and conversely inflating the positive feelings in relation to the satisfying roles/domains.

We then discussed two specific interventions that people use in value-based compensation: (1) sequencing work and nonwork goals and (2) revising existing work and nonwork goals and selecting new goals. Sequencing work and nonwork goals is a form of goal restructuring. This personal intervention involves reprioritizing goals sequentially. Specifically, work and nonwork goals are sequenced in that some goals are prioritized in the short term followed by the other goals in the longer term.

Revising or abandoning unattainable goals prevents one from fruitlessly pursuing goals likely to generate negative feelings as a result of failure.

Such intervention ensures that the revised goals (or new goals) can generate success in both domains, contributing to domain satisfaction and life satisfaction overall.

We also discussed intervention programs that organizations can institutionalize to achieve higher levels of employee work-life balance based on these personal interventions: (1) sequencing work and nonwork goals and (2) revising existing work and nonwork goals and selecting new goals.

Compare value-based compensation with another compensation strategy that we discussed in Chapter 6 – behavior-based compensation. Recall that behavior-based compensation was based on changing one's behavior rather than changing one's perception of domain importance, as was done in this chapter. Both strategies are designed to help achieve work-life balance and maintain overall life satisfaction. The underlying theoretical assumption is that dissatisfaction in any work or nonwork domain decreases overall life satisfaction. In behavior-based compensation, to compensate for a decline in life satisfaction, people engage in behaviors in other domains to increase their satisfaction in ways that can spill over. Alternatively, they cognitively change the degree of importance they assign to those domains. The dissatisfying domains become less important, and the satisfying domains become more important. Again, the theoretical assumption here is that overall life satisfaction is strongly influenced not only by domain satisfaction (satisfaction with work life, satisfaction with family life, satisfaction with social life, etc.) but also by the perceived importance of these domains. Hence, the degree of satisfaction (or dissatisfaction) the individual experiences in a life domain is amplified by the degree of importance they place on that domain. Satisfaction is amplified in domains that are more important than those perceived as less important. Conversely, dissatisfaction is amplified in domains that are more important compared to those domains perceived as less important. This is the essence of value-based compensation – an effective personal intervention to achieve work-life balance and maintain an acceptable level of life satisfaction.

In the next chapter we discuss our final work-life balance intervention, namely the whole-life perspective. This is also a cognition-based personal intervention that serves to maintain work-life balance and an acceptable level of overall life satisfaction by prompting the individual to make decisions about a contemplated course of action guided by anticipating the positive and negative consequences – not only in relation to the target role and domain but also in relation to other roles and domains.

References

Brandstätter, V., Herrmann, M., & Schüler, J. (2013). The struggle of giving up personal goals: Affective, physiological, and cognitive consequences of an action crisis. *Personality and Social Psychology Bulletin*, 39(12), 1668–1682.

Edwards, J. R. & Rothbard, N. P. (2000). Mechanisms linking work and family: Clarifying the relationship between work and family constructs. *Academy of Management Review*, 25(1), 178–199.

Greenhaus, J. H., Collins, K. M., & Shaw, J. D. (2003). The relation between work-family balance and quality of life. *Journal of Vocational Behavior*, 63(3), 510–531.

Hirschi, A., Shockley, K. M., & Zacher, H. (2019). Achieving work-family balance: An action regulation model. *Academy of Management Review*, 44(1), 150–171.

Johnson, R. E., Chang, C. H., & Lord, R. G. (2006). Moving from cognition to behavior: What the research says. *Psychological Bulletin*, 132(3): 381–415.

Lee, D.-J. & Sirgy, M. J. (2018). What do people do to achieve work-life balance? A formative conceptualization to help develop a metric for large-scale quality-of-life surveys. *Social Indicators Research*, 138(2), 771–791.

Sirgy, M. J. (2002). *The psychology of quality of life*. Dordrecht: Kluwer Academic Publishers.

Sirgy, M. J. & Lee, D.-J. (2016). Work-life balance: A quality-of-life model. *Applied Research in Quality of Life*, 11(4), 1059–1082.

Wrosch, C., Scheier, M. F., Miller, G. E., Schulz, R., & Carver, C. S. (2003). Adaptive self-regulation of unattainable goals: Goal disengagement, goal reengagement, and subjective well-being. *Personality and Social Psychology Bulletin*, 29(12), 1494–1508.

CHAPTER 12

Applying Whole-Life Perspective in Decision-Making

12.1 Applying Whole-Life Perspective in Decision-Making

Some people make work decisions about a course of action by anticipating the consequences of that action narrowly (i.e., consequences related to work life), whereas others make work decisions by anticipating the consequences of that action *more broadly* (i.e., consequences related to work and nonwork domains). The latter decision-making strategy is referred to as "whole-life perspective" and is a proven strategy to help achieve work-life balance (e.g., Briscoe, Hall, & DeMuth, 2006; Direnzo, Greenhaus & Weer, 2015; Lee & Sirgy, 2018; Powell & Greenhaus, 2012). In other words, individuals making work-life decisions (e.g., decisions about career development) using a whole-life perspective, frame these decisions broadly enough to recognize that these decisions can have an impact on nonwork domains. Here is a sample of survey items designed to capture the tendency to use a whole-life perspective in making decisions related to work life: "I strive to be successful in many different parts of my life" and "I make work-related decisions based on the effects the decisions have on many other parts of my life" (Direnzo, Greenhaus, & Weer, 2015).

Correspondingly, work-life decisions (e.g., accepting a job offer, accepting a promotion, relocating for work, starting a business, deciding on the number of hours to work every day of the work week, quitting one's job, and so on) are very much influenced by many factors in nonwork domains (e.g., family life, social life, financial life, …). For example, Powell and Greenhaus (2012) were able to empirically demonstrate that individuals make job-related decisions (e.g., whether to start a business, how many hours to devote to one's job, and whether to quit one's job) by considering family-related factors in their decision-making. Specifically, they found that individuals consider a host of family factors such as family structure, family demands and responsibilities, family support, family background, and family-related motives.

As such, Greenhaus and Powell (2012) introduced the concept of "family-relatedness" of work-life decisions and defined it as "the extent to which an individual's decision-making process and choice of a course of action in the work domain are influenced by a family situation in order to foster a positive outcome for the family (p. 247). They also made the case that the extent to which family-relatedness influences work-life decisions is moderated by contextual factors at the individual level (e.g., strength of identification with family relationships), organizational level (e.g., work demands and family-supportiveness of the workplace), and societal level (e.g., social and institutional support for meeting family responsibilities in the national culture).

Direnzo, Greenhaus, and Weer (2015) further expanded the concept of family-relatedness and transformed it into the concept of "whole-life perspective." That is, individuals with a "whole-life perspective" consider a host of nonwork factors (e.g., family, marital, financial, social, leisure, health, among other factors) in their work-life decisions – not only family factors.

How can employees implement whole-life perspective in decision-making? They can effectively implement a whole-life perspective strategy to achieve work-life balance by (1) evoking multiple identities in work-life decisions, (2) framing work-life decisions broadly, and (3) applying broadened rules to guide work-life decisions.

12.1.1 Evoking Multiple Identities in Work-Life Decisions

Direnzo, Greenhaus, and Weer (2015) elaborated on the cognitive mechanism related to whole-life perspective decision-making. They asserted that this approach to decision-making is grounded in identity theory. That is, when making work-life decisions, people are influenced by their socially constructed identities.

Individuals hold multiple socially constructed identities that reflect different roles in different life domains (e.g., parent role in family life, employee role in work life, spouse role in marital life) that collectively make up their self-concept. Identity theory asserts that people spend much more time, energy, and other resources in roles and domains that are highly salient because emotionally laden experiences in highly salient roles and domains serve to validate personal identity. People are motivated to form, hold, and validate a self-concept – or what personality psychologists have long referred to as "self-theory" (Epstein, 1973; Sirgy, 1986).

Specifically, Epstein (1973) theorized that the self-concept consists of concepts that are hierarchically organized and internally consistent about the person. It is an object of knowledge that is dynamic, yet it serves to maintain stability; it is unified and differentiated at the same time; it is used to solve problems in the real world; and it is subject to collapse, clinically speaking. As such, the self-concept is a self-theory. It is a theory that the individual has constructed about oneself, and it is part of a broader theory that they hold about an entire range of significant life experiences. As such, self-theory is a conceptual tool used to optimize the pleasure/pain balance of the individual over the course of a lifetime. Self-theory serves to facilitate the maintenance of self-esteem and organize the data of experience in a manner that helps the individual cope and deal with reality. Hence, the collapse of self-theory causes psychopathology, possibly in the form of acute schizophrenia or psychosis.

The individual is akin to a scientist who attempts to solve problems by continuously developing and testing hypotheses and revising their concepts accordingly. Both the scientist and the individual organize their observations into schemata, which are then organized into a network of broader schemata. These broader networks are essentially "theories." Thus, the data of experience are organized in a self-theory, which in turn influences the formation and maintenance of a broader theory reflecting how the person views the world at large.

An important distinction between a scientist and a layperson is the degree of objectivity in the formation, testing, and revision of concepts. Laypeople construct and revise their own self-concept motivated by the need for self-esteem and self-consistency. That is, they do so in ways that make themselves more desirable (i.e., to meet the need for self-esteem) and to reinforce the initial views they have of themselves (i.e., to meet the need for self-consistency). Hence, the layperson is less objective than the scientist.[1]

Whole-life perspective comes to bear in that people make decisions in the context of multiple identities that are linked by a coherent self-theory. As such, a decision is made in the context of one particular identity (e.g., the work identity) with a consciousness of other identities (e.g., the family identity). The extent to which a self-concept involving work and nonwork identities would be evoked to guide work-life decision-making is subject to how the individual would anticipate consequences that have a direct

---

[1] In elucidating on self-theory, one of the coauthors of this book (Sirgy, 1986) further theorized that laypeople are not only motivated by the needs for self-esteem and self-consistency but also by self-knowledge. That is, there is an inherent drive to seek information about oneself to better understand one's social roles and how to best meet role demand. This need for self-knowledge is also biased by the needs for self-esteem and self-consistency.

bearing on the needs for self-esteem and self-consistency. Consider the following case of Amanda, who is a social worker at a rehab center. Most of her clients are elderly patients who become sick or disabled and end up at the rehab center by necessity. Amanda is overwhelmed at work. She has a huge caseload, and she feels like a failure. She feels helpless to provide meaningful assistance to many of her sick and disabled patients. She also has a family – three children and a husband. She also feels like a failure as a mother and wife. She cannot fully meet the needs of her children and her husband because of her huge caseload at work. Her husband is also not sympathetic; he has old-fashion beliefs about "good" mothers and wives. He has voiced many complaints about the fact that she is neglecting her family and home duties.

Recently, she ran into a colleague and friend (Melissa) who is working at a nonprofit agency that assists the elderly and disabled. The basic mission of the agency is to help clients by assembling a complete benefit package from a number of government agencies such as the Social Security Administration, Medicare, Medicaid, Veterans Administration, Disability Insurance, and various health insurance companies (entitlement programs available in the United States). Amanda confided in Melissa about her work and family problems. Melissa recognized that there was an opportunity to recruit Amanda to her nonprofit agency, and she made her an offer. Amanda decided to accept that offer. In making this decision, she adopted a whole-life perspective by considering the consequences of that decision not only on her career development (i.e., work life) but also on meeting family demand (i.e., family life). This position would allow her to put her social work knowledge and skills to better use by helping individual clients and enhancing many aspects of their wellbeing. As such, this new position is likely to boost her self-esteem. Accepting this position is also very consistent with her personal identity of being a social worker, a wife, and mother; doing so should meet her need for self-consistency.

12.1.2   *Framing Work-Life Decisions Broadly*

Whole-life perspective also involves how decisions are framed. How a decision is framed guides the individual to seek certain types of information. The frame that is activated in a given situation plays an important role in work-life decision-making. Specifically, a work-life decision could be framed narrowly as having implications only for one's work life, or it may be framed more broadly as having implications for one's family life, social life, leisure life, etc. (Direnzo, Greenhaus, & Weer, 2015).

Going back to Amanda. By applying the whole-life perspective in considering this new position in the non-profit agency, Amanda framed the decision broadly: "How will accepting this new position affect my life at large – my career, my family, and my marriage?" She did not frame it narrowly as in: "How will this new job affect my career, period?" This broader frame helped her make a better decision that will help her achieve better work-life balance and enhance her satisfaction with life overall.

12.1.3   Applying Broadened Rules to Guide Work-Life Decisions

In applying the whole-life perspective in work-life decision-making the individual evokes certain rules. These rules help in decision-making. For example, "always discuss a work decision that may affect my family with my spouse" is a rule consistent with the whole-life perspective. In contrast, a work-life decision, such as "always accept new assignments if I think they are likely to help develop my career," is a rule inconsistent with the whole-life perspective because it leads the individual to consider the consequences more narrowly (i.e., work life only).

In the case of Amanda, she applied a rule consistent with the whole-life perspective of "always discuss a work decision that may affect my family with my spouse." As such, we need to recognize that people use a variety of decision rules that help them make work-life decisions. To help achieve greater work-life balance, employees should apply decision rules consistent with the whole-life perspective (Direnzo, Greenhaus, & Weer, 2015).

12.2   Developing a Training Program Guided by the Principle of Whole-Life Perspective

As suggested above, the whole-life perspective involves (1) evoking multiple identities in work-life decisions, (2) framing work-life decisions broadly, and (3) applying broadened rules to guide work-life decisions. Doing so facilitates work-life balance, which in turn serves to contribute to life satisfaction (see Table 12.1).

How could a work-life balance instructor apply the *multiple identities principle* in the context of an employee workshop? Perhaps the instructor can present Amanda's case to the workshop participants. In doing so, the instructor can present Table 12.2 and illustrate Amanda's decision-making using that table.

Table 12.1 *Applying the whole-life perspective in decision-making*

Intervention	Description	References
Evoking multiple identities in work-life decisions	Whole-life perspective involves multiple rather than single identities in making work-life decisions.	Direnzo, Greenhaus, and Weer (2015)
Framing work-life decisions broadly	Whole-life perspective involves the use of broadened rather than narrow frames in making decisions about work.	Direnzo, Greenhaus, and Weer (2015)
Applying broadened rules to guide work-life decisions	In applying the whole-life perspective in work-life decision-making the individual uses broadened rather than narrow rules.	Direnzo, Greenhaus, and Weer (2015)

As shown in the table, Amanda has expressed her dissatisfaction with her identity as a social worker ("–3"), her dissatisfaction with her identity as a mother ("–2"), and her dissatisfaction with her identity as a wife ("–3"). She anticipates that her dissatisfaction with her identity as a social worker will jump from "–3" to "+3" because she anticipates that her identity as a social worker will blossom in this new position. She also believes that her dissatisfaction with her identity as a mother will change from "–2" to "+3" because she will have more time at home and will be more effective in catering to her children's needs in this new position. Lastly but equally important is her identity as a wife. She believes that taking on this new position will make her husband prouder of her; he will also feel better about her role as a mother because she will devote more time and attention to their children; and finally, she believes that taking on this position is likely to strengthen her relationship with her husband, romantically. As such, she anticipates that her current level of satisfaction as a wife will change from "–3" to "+4." This is a good illustration of the whole-life perspective in work-life decision-making.

After going through Amanda's case, the instructor could then provide the participants with a template that looks like Table 12.3. Participants are then asked to complete the table by considering a work-life decision of their own – a decision they have been pondering. That is, they should list those identities that may be influenced by the contemplated decision and rate their current level of satisfaction with those identities. Then they should consider possible consequences that may impact these identities and rate the anticipated change of satisfaction given the contemplated course of action. After doing this, the instructor may wish to encourage the workshop participants to discuss their own cases to further reinforce learning.

Table 12.2 *How did Amanda go about making her work-life decision using multiple identities*

Life Domain	Relevant Identities	Current Level of Satisfaction with Identity	Anticipated Level of Satisfaction with Identity Given the Decision	Why?
Work life	Her identity of being a social worker	−3	+3	She believes that her identity as a social worker will blossom in this new position.
Family life	Her identity of being a mother	−2	+3	She will be a better mother and more effective in catering to her children's needs in this new position.
Marital life	Her identity of being a wife	−3	+4	She believes that her husband will feel proud of her for taking this new position; he will also perceive her as a better mother; and most importantly, she will be able to spend more quality time with her husband, which will strengthen their marital bond.
Narrow decision		−3	+3	She makes a decision based on considering its impact on work life only.
Broad decision		−8	+10	She makes a decision based on considering its impact on work life, family life, and marital life.

Notes:
- **Current Level of Satisfaction with Identity:** 11-point rating scale: "−5 = Very Dissatisfied"; "+5 = Very Satisfied"
- **Anticipated Level of Satisfaction with Identity Given the Decision:** 11-point rating scale: "−5 = Very Dissatisfied"; "+5 = Very Satisfied"

Table 12.3 *Applying the multiple identities principle of the whole-life perspective in decision-making*

Life Domain	Relevant Identities	Current Level of Satisfaction with Identity	Anticipated Level of Satisfaction with Identity Given the Decision	Why?
	Identity	...	...	....
	Identity	...	...	....
	Identity	...	...	....

Notes:
- **Current Level of Satisfaction with Identity:** 11-point rating scale: "−5 = Very Dissatisfied"; "+5 = Very Satisfied"
- **Anticipated Level of Satisfaction with Identity Given the Decision:** 11-point rating scale: "−5 = Very Dissatisfied"; "+5 = Very Satisfied"

We also suggest that the *broad framing* principle can be operationalized into a training module. The instructor can revisit Amanda's case with the workshop participants. In doing so, the instructor can present Table 12.4 and illustrate Amanda's decision-making using that table.

To remind the reader, we used the following framing example in Amanda's case. Amanda had a choice to frame the work-life decision broadly or narrowly. "How will accepting this new position affect my life at large – my career, my family, and my marriage?" is an example of framing the decision broadly. In contrast, "how will this new job affect my career, period?" is an example of narrow framing. Amanda has chosen to frame the decision broadly. Prompting Amanda to frame the decision both narrowly and broadly, she was able to better project how the decision is likely to impact her overall – how satisfied she is likely to be given the contemplated course of action. When she frames the decision narrowly, she anticipates that the new position can contribute *moderately* to her overall life satisfaction (an increase from "−3" to "+1") because she will be able to effectively perform this job and make a difference in the lives of her clients. This will make her happier in her work life and being happier in her work life should contribute somewhat to her overall life satisfaction. However, when she frames the decision broadly, she anticipates that the new position can contribute *significantly* to her overall life satisfaction (an increase from "−3" to "+3") because she anticipates that this new position can significantly increase her overall life satisfaction. The new position would serve not only to increase satisfaction in her work life but also in relation to her family life and marital life too. Increasing satisfaction in her work, family, and marital domains should contribute significantly to her overall life satisfaction.

Table 12.4 *How did Amanda go about making her work-life decision by framing the decision broadly*

Relevant Frames	Operationalizing the Frame	Current Level of Life Satisfaction	Anticipated Level of Life Satisfaction Given the Decision	Why?
Broad framing of the decision	How will accepting this new position affect my life at large – my career, my family, and my marriage?	−3	+3	She believes that this new position can significantly increase her overall life satisfaction because it serves not only to increase satisfaction in her work life but also in relation to her family life and marital life too.
Narrow framing of the decision	How will this new job affect my career, period?	−3	+1	She believes that the new position can contribute to her overall life satisfaction because she will be able to effectively perform this job and make a difference in the lives of her clients. This will make her happier in her work life.

Notes:
• **Current Level of Life Satisfaction:** 11-point rating scale: " −5 = Very Dissatisfied"; "+5 = Very Satisfied"
• **Anticipated Level of Life Satisfaction Given the Decision** = 11-point rating scale: " −5 = Very Dissatisfied"; "+5 = Very Satisfied"

Table 12.5 *Applying the broad framing principle of the whole-life perspective in decision-making*

Relevant Frames	Operationalizing the Frame	Current Level of Life Satisfaction	Anticipated Level of Life Satisfaction Given the Decision	Why?
Broad framing of the decision	....	...	...	......
Narrow framing of the decision	....	...	...	......

Notes:
- **Current Level of Life Satisfaction:** 11-point rating scale: "–5 = Very Dissatisfied"; "+5 = Very Satisfied"
- **Anticipated Level of Life Satisfaction Given the Decision** = 11-point rating scale: "–5 = Very Dissatisfied"; "+5 = Very Satisfied"

As such, by prompting the workshop participants to frame their work-life decision both broadly and narrowly, they can better assess the impact of the decision on work-life balance and ultimately their life satisfaction. The contrast between narrow and broad framing of the decision should better help them understand and appreciate the implications of the broad frame on work-life balance. Accordingly, we recommend that the instructor illustrate Amanda's case using Table 12.4, after which they would present Table 12.5 for the workshop participants to complete on their own. After this exercise, the instructor would encourage the participants to discuss how they completed the table to reinforce their learning.

Finally, we have the *broadened rules* principle. How can this principle be operationalized into a training module? The instructor can again revisit Amanda's case with the workshop participants. In doing so, the instructor can present Table 12.6 and illustrate Amanda's decision-making using that table. As a friendly reminder, Amanda applied a rule consistent with the whole-life perspective of "always discuss a work decision that may affect my family with my spouse." Additionally, we need to recognize that people use a variety of decision rules that help them make work-life decisions.

The table pits two decision rules against each other: narrow versus broad. If the broad decision rule ("always discuss a work decision that may affect my family with my spouse") were to be applied, Amanda anticipates that her life satisfaction will increase by a large margin ("+4" on an 11-point rating scale – see Notes in Table 12.6). Specifically, discussing it with her husband is likely to help her consider how the new position will impact her family life, her marital life, as well as her own career development.

Table 12.6 *How did Amanda go about making her work-life*
decision by using broadened decision rules

Relevant Decision Rules	Operationalizing the Rule	Will the Rule Impact Life Satisfaction?	How?
Broad decision rule	Always discuss a work decision that may affect family with her spouse.	+4	Discussing the decision with her husband is likely to help her consider how the new position will impact her family life, her marital life, as well as her own career development. She anticipates that after discussing it with her husband, the new position can significantly increase her overall life satisfaction because it is likely to serve not only to increase satisfaction in her work life but also in relation to her family life and marital life.
Narrow decision rule	Always take on new projects likely to help boost her career.	+1	Taking on this new position is likely to boost her career, which in turn will make her happier in her work life. The overall result is a moderate boost in her life satisfaction.

Notes:
• **Will the Rule Affect Life Satisfaction?** 11-point rating scale: "−5 = Decrease Life Satisfaction by a Huge Margin"; "+5 = Increase Life Satisfaction by a Huge Margin"

She anticipates that the new position can significantly increase her overall life satisfaction because it is likely to serve not only to increase satisfaction in her work life but also in relation to her family life and marital life. In contrast, if the narrow decision rule ("Always take on new projects likely to help boost her career") were to be applied, Amanda anticipates that her life satisfaction will increase by a moderate amount ("+1" on an 11-point rating scale varying from "−5" to "+5"). This is because taking on this new position is likely to boost her career, which in turn will make her happier in her work life. The overall result is a moderate boost in her life satisfaction.

As we have done in examining this framing principle, the instructor could prompt the workshop participants to use two decision rules, one broad and the other narrow. Doing so should allow them to assess the impact of implementing these decision rules on their work-life balance and life satisfaction. The contrast between narrow and broad decision rules should help

Table 12.7 *Applying the broad rule principle of the whole-life perspective in decision-making*

Relevant Decision Rules	Operationalizing the Rule	Will the Rule Impact Life Satisfaction?	How?
Broad decision rule	....	...	....
Narrow decision rule	....	...	....

Notes:
- **Will the Rule Affect Life Satisfaction?** 11-point rating scale: "–5 = Decrease Life Satisfaction by a Huge Margin"; "+5 = Increase Life Satisfaction by a Huge Margin"

them better understand and appreciate the implications of applying these decision rules on work-life balance. Accordingly, we recommend that the instructor illustrate Amanda's case using Table 12.6, after which they would present Table 12.7 for the workshop participants to complete on their own. After this exercise, the instructor would encourage the participants to discuss how they completed the table to reinforce their learning.

12.3 Conclusion

In this chapter we described a cognitive, personal intervention of work-life balance referred to as whole-life perspective. This is an approach to decision-making that considers possible consequences in work and non-work life domains. As such, we made the distinction between broad versus narrow decision-making. Narrow decision-making is the type of decision-making that considers the consequences of the contemplated course of action narrowly (i.e., possible consequences related to work life), whereas broad decision-making considers possible consequences related to both work and nonwork domains. A whole-life perspective approach to decision-making is best captured by having survey respondents endorse a statement such as "I make work-related decisions based on the effects the decisions have on many other parts of my life."

We then discussed how the whole-life perspective in decision-making is implemented. We identified three methods: (1) evoking multiple identities in work-life decisions, (2) framing work-life decisions broadly, and (3) applying broadened rules to guide work-life decisions.

People make whole-life perspective decisions by evoking multiple identities that are linked by a coherent self-concept. A work-life decision is made in the context of the work identity with a consciousness of other identities (e.g., the family identity). A whole-life perspective also involves how decisions are framed. A work-life decision could be framed narrowly as having implications only for one's work life, or it may be framed more broadly as having implications for one's family life, social life, leisure life, etc. Lastly, in applying the whole-life perspective in work-life decision-making the individual evokes certain rules. Some rules are more consistent with a whole-life perspective than others. "Always discuss a work decision that may affect my family with my spouse" is a rule consistent with the whole-life perspective. In contrast, "Always accept new assignments if I think they are likely to help develop my career" is a rule inconsistent with the whole-life perspective because it leads the individual to consider the consequences more narrowly (i.e., work life only).

We also discussed how instructors can use these three whole-life perspective principles to train employees to achieve greater work-life balance. Training employees to achieve work-life balance is key here, and applying the whole-life perspective to decision-making is imperative.

References

Briscoe, J. P., Hall, D. T., & DeMuth, R. L. F. (2006). Protean and boundaryless careers: An empirical exploration. *Journal of Vocational Behavior*, 69(1), 30–47.

Direnzo, M. S., Greenhaus, J. H., & Weer, C. H. (2015). Relationship between protean career orientation and work-life balance: A resource perspective. *Journal of Organizational Behavior*, 36(4), 538–560.

Epstein, S. (1973). The self-concept revisited: Or a theory of a theory. *American Psychologist*, 28(5), 404–414.

Greenhaus, J. H. & Powell, G. N. (2012). The family-relatedness of work decisions: A framework and agenda for theory and research. *Journal of Vocational Behavior*, 80(3), 246–255.

Lee, D.-J. & Sirgy, M. J. (2018). What do people do to achieve work-life balance? A formative conceptualization to help develop a metric for large-scale quality-of-life surveys. *Social Indicators Research*, 138(2), 771–791.

Powell, G. N. & Greenhaus, J. H. (2012). When family considerations influence work decisions: Decision-making processes. *Journal of Vocational Behavior*, 81(3), 322–329.

Sirgy, M. J. (1986). *Self-congruity: Toward a theory of personality and cybernetics.* New York: Praeger Publishers/Greenwood Publishing Group.

PART IV

Epilogue

The core contribution of this book lies in the personal interventions that employees can learn to apply to achieve work-life balance, covered in Parts II and III. In these two parts of the book, we discussed nine personal interventions – five behavior-based personal interventions and another four cognition-based life domain interventions. The behavior-based strategies were (1) engaging in multiple roles and domains, (2) increasing role enrichment, (3) engaging in behavior-based compensation, (4) managing role conflict, and (5) creating role balance. The cognition-based strategies were (6) segmenting roles and domains, (7) integrating roles and domains, (8)

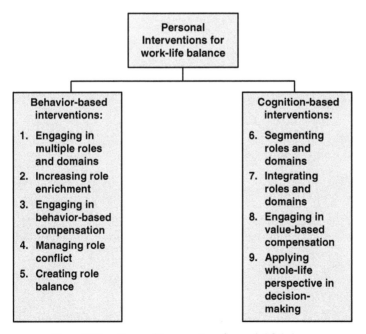

Figure PIV.1   Personal interventions for work-life balance

engaging in value-based compensation, and (9) applying whole-life per-spective in decision-making (see Figure PIV.1).

We wrap up in Part IV of the book (Chapter 13) by summarizing the nine principles of work-life balance and the personal interventions guided by these principles.

CHAPTER 13

Conclusion

13.1 Part I of the Book

In Part I (Chapters 1–3) we described the conceptual foundation of the research on work-life balance. In Chapter 1 we provided the reader with several definitions of work-life balance, namely (1) equal engagement and satisfaction in work and nonwork domains, (2) engagement in work and nonwork roles compatible with life goals, (3) successful accomplishment of goals in work and nonwork domains, (4) full engagement in multiple life domains, and (5) minimal role conflict between work and nonwork life domains.

Equal engagement and satisfaction in work and nonwork domains mean that work-life balance is achieved when employees become equally engaged and satisfied with work and nonwork roles. That is, work-life balance is viewed in terms of an individual's perceptions of the degree of balance in time, involvement, and satisfaction in work and nonwork life domains. The second definition of work-life balance (engagement in work and nonwork roles compatible with life goals) focuses on the extent to which an individual's effectiveness and satisfaction in work and family roles are compatible with the individual's life role priorities at a given point in time. The third definition (successful accomplishment of goals in work and nonwork domains) focuses on the successful accomplishment of goals in both work and nonwork domains. That is, work-life balance is experienced when the individual is not only fully engaged in work and nonwork roles but also successfully meeting their role-related expectations. The fourth definition (full engagement in multiple life domains) focuses on full engagement in each of the roles assumed. That is, work-life balance is achieved when people are fully committed in their various social roles in work and nonwork life. The fifth and last definition (minimal role conflict between work and nonwork domains) focuses on role conflict and how to decrease it. That is, individuals with work-life balance tend to experience minimal role conflict between work and nonwork life domains – the successful management of role conflict across life domains.

We made the case in Chapter 2 that work-life balance is an important topic for all organizations. Substantial research has shown that work-life balance influences a host of organizational outcomes (e.g., organizational identification, loyalty, and commitment; turnover, job performance, employee morale, and organizational citizenship) and personal outcomes (e.g., employee stress, employee burnout, employee wellbeing, satisfaction with life overall, personal happiness, eudaimonia, satisfaction with family life, satisfaction with social life, satisfaction with leisure life, satisfaction with spiritual life, satisfaction with financial life).

In Chapter 3 we discussed much of the research that explains how work-life balance contributes significantly to life satisfaction. We provided several explanations of the direct link between work-life balance and life satisfaction. Specifically, work-life balance contributes to overall life satisfaction through satisfaction in multiple domains. That is, individuals with a balanced life tend to be fully engaged in multiple roles. Engaging in a single role does not substantially contribute to overall life satisfaction. When people become engaged in only one life domain (e.g., work life), they are not likely to experience life satisfaction because the amount of satisfaction that we can extract from a single life domain is limited. Overall, life satisfaction is mostly determined by an aggregation of satisfaction from various life domains. When employees engage in multiple social roles and have satisfied the full spectrum of development needs, they are likely to experience a high level of overall life satisfaction. Another explanation of how work-life balance contributes to life satisfaction involves positive spillover. That is, those with a balanced life are likely to experience positive spillover across life domains. Positive spillover refers to positive mood, skills, values, and behaviors that transfer from one life domain to another. Engagement in multiple roles may increase satisfaction with life overall through the transfer of positive experiences from one life domain to another. In other words, learning that occurs in one life domain is easily transferred to other life domains, thus enhancing role engagement and effectiveness in multiple domains. Yet another explanation involves minimal role conflict. That is, people who have a balanced life are less likely to experience role conflict across life domains. When individuals devote a significant portion of their time, attention, and energy to one role (e.g., work life), they are likely to experience difficulty in meeting the demands of another role (e.g., family life). In this case, they experience conflict between work life and family life. Invariably, role conflict takes a toll on life satisfaction.

Work-life balance leads to both life domain satisfaction and stress reduction. The domain satisfaction explanation posits that work-life balance contributes positively and significantly to life domain satisfaction. That is, work-life balance contributes to satisfaction in marital life, family life, health and safety, and leisure life.

Poor work-life balance is also associated with the following stress-related outcomes, namely, emotional exhaustion, psychological distress, and bad mental health. Imbalanced employees tend to experience burnout more often than balanced employees. The burnout may be due to work-family conflict and is indicated by symptoms of emotional exhaustion. Marital and parental distress and anxiety also result from work-family conflict. Work-life imbalance is also associated with depression.

13.2   Part II of the Book

In the second part of the book (Chapters 4–8) we described five personal interventions that people commonly used to achieve work-life balance, namely (1) engaging in multiple roles and domains, (2) increasing role enrichment, (3) engaging in behavior-based compensation, (4) managing role conflict, and (5) creating role balance. These personal interventions are behavior-based. In contrast, we described other personal interventions in Part III that are cognition-based. We made the case that the distinction between behavior-based personal interventions of work-life balance and cognition-based interventions is a matter of degree rather than a categorical difference. That is, behavior-based interventions are mostly interventions initiated by some explicit behavior. The converse applies to cognition-based interventions: they involve a mental process. That is not to say the mental process does not involve some explicit behavior. In many cases, cognition-based interventions are manifested in terms of explicit behaviors.

With respect to the first personal intervention (engaging in multiple roles and domains), we argued that active involvement in social roles of various life domains is imperative to work-life balance and life satisfaction. Engagement in multiple life domains is likely to ensure successful role performance, which in turn contributes to domain satisfaction resulting in overall life satisfaction. People can only obtain a limited amount of satisfaction from a single life domain. As such, to feel satisfied with life overall, people have to feel satisfied with their entire spectrum of needs (basic needs such as food and shelter, and growth needs such as social, esteem, and self-actualization needs). We also discussed how role engagement is commonly implemented through three types of personal interventions: (1) increasing role involvement in a manner consistent with life values, (2) engaging in multiple domains to achieve positive balance, and (3) engaging in important roles with harmonious passion. With respect to increasing role involvement in a manner consistent with life values, individuals evaluate life goals and invest enough resources to achieve those goals. They evaluate their values and priorities related to a role in a life domain and adjust allotted time and energy to the role based on these values and priorities.

With respect to engaging in multiple life domains to achieve positive balance, people engage in multiple life domains that have high personal relevance in order to achieve positive balance. Positive balance means that life satisfaction can be increased by acceptable role performance in multiple important life domains, rather than maximizing satisfaction in a single domain. Achieving moderate-to-high satisfaction in several life domains that are important to the individual (e.g., work life, family life, financial life) works best to boost life satisfaction. Thus, "positive" in "positive balance" reflects "moderate-to-high levels of domain satisfaction," whereas "balance" refers to the idea of achieving comparable "moderate-to-high levels of satisfaction" in several important life domains.

The third intervention in role engagement to help achieve work-life balance is engagement in important roles with harmonious passion. We made the distinction between harmonious passion and obsessive passion. When activities become internalized in a person's identity, they reflect either harmonious passion or obsessive passion. A person who engages in a role with harmonious passion tends to identify with that role in an autonomous manner and with a sense of control. In contrast, obsessive passion lacks autonomy. "Workaholics" is a good term to characterize obsessive passion in work life.

We also discussed how a training program can be developed reflecting these three principles underlying role engagement. That is, workshops and seminars can be developed and offered to employees to help them achieve work-life balance through role engagement.

With respect to the second personal intervention (increasing role enrichment), we describe how individuals enrich their roles by transferring their skills, psychological capital, and social capital from one role to the next in work and nonwork domains. Individuals experience role enrichment when involvement in one life domain (e.g., work life) helps them understand different viewpoints and develop knowledge, skills, and capabilities in other life domains (e.g., family life). Role enrichment can be increased through the use of skills, psychological capital, and social capital across all life domains. That is, people apply the skills they use at work in nonwork domains such as family life. Individuals also use psychological capital across life domains.

Psychological capital refers to positive mental traits people build over time enhancing role performance (e.g., self-esteem, self-confidence, optimism, openness to experience, conscientiousness, social intelligence, and emotional intelligence). Roles can be enriched by transferring these positive psychological traits from one role to another and one life domain to another. The use of social capital across life domains is yet another strategy of role enrichment. Social capital refers to interpersonal skills and social networks. Social capital contributes to role enrichment in significant ways, and that role enrichment plays a significant part in work-life balance and life satisfaction. Guided by our understanding of the role enrichment principles, we developed pedagogical material that can be used by instructors of work-life balance to help employees through a training seminar or workshop.

The third personal intervention (engaging in behavior-based compensation) focuses on how people try to maintain an acceptable level of life satisfaction by engaging in behaviors in roles and life domains that can produce more happiness. Conversely, they decrease their involvement in roles and domains that are dissatisfying. In other words, behavior-based compensation means decreased engagement in a dissatisfying role/domain, coupled with an increased engagement in alternative roles/domains that produce positive affect. These compensatory behaviors can include increases (or decreases) in the allotment of time, energy, and/or financial resources.

Reallocating *time* is a behavior-based compensation intervention in which time is reallocated to a role in which an individual has found satisfying in the past and anticipates more satisfaction through increased role engagement. That is, the person allocates more time to the satisfying role and less time to the dissatisfying role. In contrast, a person can reallocate *energy*, not time necessarily. That is, when people become dissatisfied with a specific role in a specific life domain, they compensate for the loss of satisfaction by increasing effort expended in another role or domain. A similar case can be made concerning financial resources. That is, people attempt to compensate for the dissatisfaction they experience in certain roles and domains by *spending more money* in roles and domains producing high levels of satisfaction. We then used these compensation principles to develop a training program to help employees achieve work-life balance.

In regard to the fourth personal intervention of work-life balance (managing role conflict), we described how people manage to meet role demand in multiple domains in ways that are less likely to produce psychological stress and role overload. Doing so helps guard against decreases in overall life satisfaction. People experience role conflict between work and family roles because the demands of work and family roles are inherently incompatible.

How do people manage role conflict? They do so by (1) matching role demand with role resources, (2) managing time, and (3) managing stress. Employees experience role conflict because they cannot devote enough time or energy to perform their roles successfully. To reduce role conflict, people have to *match role demand and resources* across life domains. Role conflict also frequently occurs when *time* demands associated with participation in one role interfere with participation in another role. That is, problems arising from scheduling the amount of time devoted to work or family roles or both is work-family conflict. Finally, role conflict is also managed by reducing *stress*. We discussed several stress management techniques such as regular exercise, meditation and praying, and social support. We also discussed how we can translate the principles of managing role conflict into training modules that can be implemented by instructors of work-life balance.

The fifth and last behavior-based personal intervention of work-life balance we discussed was creating role balance. This intervention involves engaging in balanced activities – balance between activities designed to maintain role function and activities designed to allow the individual to flourish in a specific work or nonwork role. People engage in maintenance activities in work and nonwork roles to meet basic needs (e.g., biological and security needs). We use the term "maintenance activities" because these are a means to help the individual function in daily life. We need to function on a daily basis, and we need to function reasonably well to be able to flourish. "Flourishing activities" in work and nonwork roles serve to meet growth needs (e.g., needs for affiliation, esteem, self-actualization, knowledge, creativity, and aesthetics). As such, role balance is created by engaging in *both* maintenance and flourishing activities in work and nonwork roles.

We then described some maintenance and flourishing activities that are essential to creating role balance in work and nonwork domains. We discussed the research demonstrating that a job that fails to meet basic needs causes job dissatisfaction (negative feelings and emotions such as anger, fear, anxiety, despair, hopelessness, and depression). However, a job that meets basic needs does not contribute much to job satisfaction or positive emotions (e.g., happiness and joy). A good job that meets basic needs can provide only relief, not joy or happiness. Conversely, a job that satisfies high-order growth needs can contribute significantly to positive emotions such as happiness. A job that fails to meet high-order needs is not likely to cause much job dissatisfaction. As such, people engage in maintenance activities to meet their basic needs and ensure minimal job dissatisfaction. They also engage in flourishing activities in work life to ensure maximal job satisfaction. To reiterate, maintenance activities tend to satisfy basic needs, not growth needs. Conversely, flourishing activities involve activities designed to satisfy growth needs. We described maintenance versus flourishing activities by focusing on work and nonwork domains.

In relation to *work life*, maintenance activities could be arriving or beginning work on time every day, avoiding excessive absences, and performing job duties in a timely manner. Examples of flourishing activities in work life include setting career goals, developing concrete plans to attain career goals, and monitoring progress toward goal attainment. As such, role balance involves engaging in both maintenance and flourishing activities in a balanced manner that contribute to life satisfaction; and imbalances may cause dissatisfaction.

We discussed nonwork domains in terms of health and safety, marital life, family life, financial life, social life, leisure life, and cultural life. Examples of maintenance activities in *health and safety* include maintaining a healthy lifestyle through physical exercise and eating a well-balanced diet, having regular health checkups, and complying with doctors' orders. In contrast, examples of flourishing activities include making physical exercise a sport, making cooking a hobby, and planning social outings with nutritious meals and physical exercise. Focusing on *marital life*, we used the following example of maintenance activities: making plans to maintain one's relationship with a romantic partner, such as buying a house together. Examples of flourishing activities in marital life include taking one's spouse out for a romantic dinner, getting together with good friends as a couple, traveling with one's significant other, reminiscing about positive experiences one shared as a couple, and making love in exotic locations. Focusing on *family life*, examples of maintenance activities include childcare, schooling, meal preparation, attending to the sick, elderly care, doing household chores, and shopping for family needs, among a multitude of other essential tasks. Flourishing activities in family life include planning a family vacation, holding social events with family members, engaging in sports with family members, and engaging in leisure activities with family members. In regard to *financial life*, maintenance activities include performing a job that produces enough income to pay the bills and buy the essentials. Flourishing activities in financial life, on the other hand, may involve investing for future growth and consuming goods and services that have elements of novelty and excitement. How about *social life*? Maintenance activities in this life domain include attending important family functions such as weddings as well as funerals, supporting relatives and friends when they are sick or in need, and attending social events at work to strengthen the social bond with one's coworkers. In contrast, flourishing activities in social life include playing an exciting game with one's friends on a regular basis, going out with friends on a social outing, and joining a social club that meets regularly. With respect to *leisure life*, maintenance activities may involve engaging in leisure activities that can help the person to relax and destress. Flourishing activities may involve engagement in competitive games that allow the person to express related skills and mastery or starting a new hobby that one enjoys. The last nonwork life domain we discussed was cultural life. Examples of maintenance activities in cultural life may include traveling to places to learn about one's own culture and the culture of other people. Flourishing activities, on the other hand, may involve traveling to destinations that reflect aspects of personal identity, spirituality, and heritage; traveling to destinations to learn about the cultures of other people to expand one's knowledge and wisdom. We then discussed how instructors of work-life balance can implement the role balance principle in workshops designed to train employees on how to increase work-life balance.

13.3   Part III of the Book

To reiterate, Part II of the book focused on behavior-based interventions: engaging in multiple roles and domains, increasing role enrichment, engaging in behavior-based compensation, managing role conflict, and creating role balance. Part III of the book focused on cognition-based personal interventions of work-life balance. These are: segmenting roles and domains, integrating roles and domains, engaging in value-based compensation, and applying whole-life perspective in decision-making.

Focusing on the first cognitive-based strategy in Part III, or the sixth personal intervention (*segmenting roles and domains*), we described segmentation in terms of creating boundaries (or psychological walls) to insulate life domains. The goal is to prevent negative spillover from the segmented domain to other domains. As such, we discussed four different segmentation interventions that work-life balanced people commonly use to prevent negative spillover: temporal, physical, behavior, and communicative.

We discussed *temporal segmentation* in terms of creating time boundaries. For example, employees segment work life from interference from family life (or vice versa) by making decisions and changes in one's daily calendar. In contrast, *physical segmentation* involves physical and spatial boundaries. One can insulate a domain by making decisions to engage in domain-related activities within specified boundaries that are spatial in nature (e.g., the physical space of home becomes the boundary protecting family life). *Behavior segmentation* involves behavior-based boundaries. An example may be the use of two email accounts to separate professional from personal life. *Communicative segmentation* involves managing boundaries with others. An example is to request supervisor and coworkers not call at home to discuss job-related concerns during non-business hours. We also discussed intervention programs that organizations can institutionalize to achieve higher levels of employee work-life balance based on these segmentation interventions.

The seventh personal intervention described in this book involves *integrating roles and domains*. Segmentation works best when people experience negative feelings in one life domain that can spill over and "infect" other domains. The result can diminish overall life satisfaction. As such, segmentation was described as a personal intervention that serves to protect life satisfaction from dipping due to negative spillover. The opposite occurs with integration. Integration is commonly used to take advantage of positive feelings in one or more domains that can spill over to other life domains. There are many situations and occupations that are better off with integration rather than a segmentation type of work-life balance intervention. We used the example of entrepreneurs and owners/managers of small businesses. To be successful in their professional roles they have to adapt by integrating their work and nonwork domains.

We discussed four ways through which people integrate their life domains to achieve work-life balance: temporal integration, physical integration, behavior integration, and communicative integration. We discussed how gig work (i.e., freelance and contract work) is an example of *temporal integration* due to schedule flexibility – integrate work life with other life domains using scheduling flexibility. We also discussed *physical integration* by describing how people manipulate physical space. For example, an employee uses their place of residence to attend to job-related matters as well as personal matters. Telework is thus viewed as an integration strategy serving to decrease work-to-family conflict (the type of stress originating from work and spilling over into family life) due to increased flexibility and control over where the employee performs their job.

With respect to *behavior integration*, we made the case that integration can be achieved through actual behavior such as the use of personal connections across domains. We focused on how employees use personal connections for work purposes; and conversely how work connections are used for personal purposes. Such cross-domain use of personal resources is a key characteristic of the integration of work and nonwork roles and domains. Finally, *communicative integration* was described in terms of the use ICTs (e.g., the internet and smartphones) – how workers use ICTS to help them move from one role to another, one life domain to another, seamlessly and effortlessly.

We discussed intervention programs that organizations can institutionalize to achieve higher levels of employee work-life balance based on these personal strategies. We also discussed how organizations can develop a training program around the integration principle and encourage selected employees (only those who are likely to benefit the most such as managers) to integrate their lives by manipulating temporal, physical, behavior, and communicative elements.

With respect to the eighth personal intervention of work-life balance (*value-based compensation*), we described this intervention in terms of changing one's perceptions of the importance of work and nonwork roles and life domains. Specifically, people change their perceptions of how important a role or domain is based on how satisfied they feel about these roles/domains. They place greater value on those roles/domains they find satisfying and less value on those roles/domains they find dissatisfying. Making changes to the perceived importance of roles/domains serves to maintain an acceptable level of life satisfaction. In other words, people "compensate" for the dissatisfaction they experience in roles/domains by deflating the negative feelings in relation to the dissatisfying roles/domains and conversely inflating the positive feelings in relation to the satisfying roles/domains.

We then discussed two specific interventions that people use in value-based compensation: (1) sequencing work and nonwork goals and (2) revising existing work and nonwork goals and selecting new goals. *Sequencing work and nonwork goals* is a form of goal restructuring. This personal intervention involves reprioritizing goals sequentially. Specifically, work and nonwork goals are either prioritized in the short term or the long term, depending on goal priority coupled with progress in achieving those goals. *Revising or abandoning unattainable goals* prevents one from fruitlessly pursuing goals likely to generate negative feelings as a result of failure. Such intervention ensures that the revised goals (or new goals) can generate success in both domains contributing to domain satisfaction and life satisfaction overall. We also discussed intervention programs that organizations can institutionalize to achieve higher levels of employee work-life balance based on these personal interventions.

The last and the ninth intervention discussed in the book was *applying whole-life perspective in decision-making*. This is also a cognition-based personal intervention that serves to maintain work-life balance and an acceptable level of overall life satisfaction by prompting the individual to make decisions about a potential course of action guided by anticipating the positive and negative consequences, not only in relation to the target role and domain but also in relation to other roles and domains. That is, the whole-life perspective is an approach to decision-making that considers possible consequences in work and nonwork life domains. As such, we made the distinction between broad versus narrow decision-making. Narrow decision-making considers the consequences of the contemplated course of action narrowly (i.e., possible consequences related to work life), whereas broad decision-making considers possible consequences related to both work and nonwork domains.

We then discussed how the whole-life perspective in decision-making is implemented. We identified three approaches used in decision-making: (1) evoking multiple identities in work-life decisions, (2) framing work-life decisions broadly, and (3) applying broadened rules to guide work-life decisions. People make whole-life perspective decisions by *evoking multiple identities* that are linked by a coherent self-concept. A work-life decision is made in the context of the work identity with a consciousness of other identities (e.g., the family identity). A whole-life perspective also involves how decisions are *framed*. A work-life decision could be framed narrowly as having implications only for one's work life, or it may be framed more broadly as having implications for one's family life, social life, leisure life, etc. Lastly, in applying the whole-life perspective in work-life decision-making the individual evokes certain *rules*. Some rules are more consistent with a whole-life perspective than others. "Always discuss a work decision that may affect my family with my spouse" is a rule consistent with the whole-life perspective. In contrast, "Always accept new assignments if I think they are likely to help develop my career" is a rule inconsistent with the whole-life perspective because it forces the individual to consider the consequences more narrowly (i.e., work life only). We also discussed how instructors can use these three whole-life perspective principles to train employees to achieve greater work-life balance. Training employees to achieve work-life balance is key here, and applying the whole-life perspective to decision-making is imperative.

13.4 Concluding Thoughts

Hopefully, by now the reader will realize that work-life balance is an important dimension of wellbeing and positive mental health. Work-life balance is a state that characterizes satisfaction in work life with little or no negative affect in nonwork domains. Achieving balance between work life and nonwork domains allows people to satisfy the full spectrum of human development needs, both basic and growth needs, which in turn contributes to long-term happiness.

Martin Seligman is considered to be the father of positive psychology. Positive psychology is the scientific study of human flourishing and optimal functioning. Much of psychology today has been dominated by "negative psychology" – a study of human behavior that focuses on psychopathology and human illbeing. While "positive psychology" emphasizes the positive aspects of human behavior and wellbeing. As such, positive psychology focuses on how to help people prosper and lead happy lives. In contrast, negative psychology focuses on how to help people deal with the stresses and strains of life. Positive psychology focuses on how to enhance life satisfaction; negative psychology focuses on how to reduce life dissatisfaction. Martin Seligman wrote many books; his earlier publications focused on topics related to negative psychology such as learned helplessness (e.g., Seligman, 1972). His later publications focused on positive psychology such as authentic happiness (Seligman, 2002) and human flourishing (Seligman, 2011). Seligman (2011) has argued that there are five pillars of positive psychology, namely positive emotions, engagement, relationships, meaning, and accomplishment. That is, human flourishing is based on five major sets of experiences in life, namely, experiencing pleasure or positive emotions (the pleasant life), experiencing a high level of engagement in satisfying activities (the engaged life), experiencing positive relationships with significant others (the social life), a sense of connectedness to a greater whole (the meaningful life), and a sense of significant accomplishments (the accomplished life).

Joe Sirgy (coauthor of this book) and one of his graduate students Jiun Wu at Virginia Tech (Sirgy & Wu, 2009) built on Seligman's five dimensions of personal happiness and human flourishing by adding a sixth dimension: *the balanced life*. They argued that balance in life contributes significantly to personal happiness and human flourishing. This may be due to the fact that only a limited amount of satisfaction can be derived from a single life domain. People have to be involved in multiple domains to satisfy the full spectrum of human development needs (biological, safety, social, esteem, self-actualization, knowledge, and aesthetics needs). Different life domains tend to focus on different human development needs. More specifically, balance contributes to life satisfaction because wellbeing can only be attained when both survival (basic) and growth needs are met. In other words, high levels of life satisfaction cannot be attained with the satisfaction of basic needs or growth needs alone. Both sets of needs have to be met to contribute significantly to life satisfaction in the long run. The Sirgy and Wu (2009) article won the Best Paper Award in the *Journal of Happiness Studies* and was reprinted in *Explorations of Happiness* (edited by Delle Fave, 2013).

Dong-Jin Lee and Joe Sirgy (coauthors of this book) have used this conceptualization of work-life balance and provided much empirical evidence demonstrating that people who have work-life balance are more likely to experience higher levels of life satisfaction than those who have imbalance (Lee & Sirgy, 2018; Sirgy & Lee, 2016, 2018b). Our conceptualization of work-life balance has an important clinical implication. Balance implies that "putting all your eggs in one basket" may not be effective in increasing life satisfaction. That is, one should not allow one life domain to overwhelm one's satisfaction or dissatisfaction with life. It is best to be invested emotionally in several domains. Doing so allows the individual to compensate for the dissatisfaction of some domains with the satisfaction of other domains.

More recently, Joe Sirgy (Sirgy, 2019, 2020) developed a theory coined "positive balance." The theory is designed to integrate wellbeing concepts across a hierarchy varying from the physiological level to the social-ecological level. The theory of positive balance can be summarized as follows. Individuals with high levels of positive mental health are likely to experience: (1) a preponderance of neurochemicals related to positive emotions (dopamine, serotonin, etc.) relative to neurochemicals related to negative emotions (cortisol), at a physiological level; (2) a preponderance of positive affect (happiness, joy, etc.) relative to negative affect (anger, sadness, etc.), at an emotional level; (3) a preponderance of domain satisfaction (satisfaction in salient and multiple life domains such as family life, work life, etc.) relative to dissatisfaction in other life domains, at a cognitive level; (4) a preponderance of positive evaluations about one's life using certain standards of comparison (satisfaction with one's life compared to one's past life, the life of family members, etc.) relative to negative evaluations about one's life using similar or other standards of comparison, at a metacognitive level; (5) a preponderance of positive psychological traits (self-acceptance, personal growth, etc.) relative to negative psychological traits (pessimism, hopelessness, etc.), at a development level; and (6) a preponderance of perceived social resources (social acceptance, social actualization, etc.) relative to perceived social constraints (social exclusion, ostracism, etc.), at a social-ecological level.

As such, we submit to the readers of this book that the concept of the balanced life is not only an important concept in its own right but should also be viewed as a major pillar in the science of wellbeing and positive mental health. Work-life balance is inextricably linked with wellbeing and positive mental health concepts, such as life satisfaction, personal happiness, human flourishing, subjective wellbeing, psychological wellbeing, hedonic wellbeing, positive emotions, and perceived quality of life. Instructors conducting training in work-life balance workshops should understand that helping employees achieve work-life balance goals is key to human wellbeing and flourishing. *And science proves it!*

References

Delle Fave, A. (2013). *The exploration of happiness: Present and future perspectives.* Dordrecht: Springer.

Lee, D.-J. & Sirgy, M. J. (2018). What do people do to achieve work-life balance? A formative conceptualization to help develop a metric for large-scale quality-of-life surveys. *Social Indicators Research*, 138(2), 771–791.

Seligman, M. E. P. (1972). Learned helplessness. *Annual Review of Medicine*, 23(1), 407–412.

Seligman, M. E. P. (2002). *Authentic happiness: Using the new positive psychology to realize your potential for lasting fulfillment.* New York: Simon and Schuster.

Seligman, M. E. P. (2011). *Flourish: A visionary new understanding of happiness and well-being.* New York: Free Press.

Sirgy, M. J. (2019). Positive balance: A hierarchical perspective of positive mental health. *Quality of Life Research*, 28(7), 1921–1930.

Sirgy, M. J. (2020). *Positive balance: A theory of well-being and positive mental health.* Dordrecht: Springer.

Sirgy, M. J. & Lee, D.-J. (2016). Work-life balance: A quality-of-life model. *Applied Research in Quality of Life*, 11(4), 1059–1082.

Sirgy, M. J. & Lee, D.-J. (2018a). Work-life balance: An integrative review. *Applied Research in Quality of Life*, 13(1), 229–254.

Sirgy, M. J. & Lee, D.-J. (2018b). The psychology of life balance. In E. Diener, S. Oishi, & L. Tay (Eds.), *e-Handbook of well-being, Noba scholar handbook series: Subjective well-being.* Salt Lake City: DEF Publishers. https://nobascholar.com.

Sirgy, M. J. & Wu, J. (2009). The pleasant life, the engaged life, and the meaningful life: What about the balanced life? *Journal of Happiness Studies*, 10(2), 183–196.

Index

CPSIA information can be obtained
at www.ICGtesting.com
Printed in the USA
BVHW052314220123
656884BV00026B/429